# Create Work You Love

Nancy Hanson

Dear
Cathi,

Thank-you
for your
Support!
Aloha,
Nancy

P.S. Betty Moore
Loves You!!!
☺

For my dad who loved
not only his work; he loved life.

# CONTENTS

# ACKNOWLEDGEMENTS

To quote literary agent and author of *How to Write a Book Proposal*, Michael Larsen, "Although I accept full responsibility for this book's faults, I am grateful to be able to share with a multitude any praise for its virtues."

Thank you to …

Ed Colozzi who taught me so much about career planning.

All the people who love their work who have shared their stories in this book.

All the students from Chaminade University who have taken the Career Development class. Thank you for discovering so many people who love their work and sharing their stories.

Jana Wolff for her editing, and even more, for her support and friendship.

Joanie Adams, Annabel Chotzen, Sam Horn, Susan Luke, and Susanne Sims. You know the special support you have given and I thank you.

Bea Borden, Kate Muller, Paula Prevost, and Pat Wataoka for their help in editing, typing, and cheerleading.

All the staff at Kinkos, Carol March and Erik Tomita at New Tech Imaging, Dale Vermeer for the grrreat cover, and Nancy Porter for the grrreat layout.

My mom, Barbara, and my husband, Jerol – the best mom and the best husband in the world.

The still small voice that leads and guides.

# INTRODUCTION

Welcome to *Create Work You Love*. As a career counselor, I see people who do not think it is possible to create enjoyable work. I am here to tell you that it is possible.

The purpose of this book is to inspire you to continue or start creating work you love. You will read about those who love their work and you will get steps to start your own love-job journey.

Look at the career planning shelf in any bookstore and notice the excellent supply of books on how to: write a great resume, interview, dress for success, and discover the hidden job market. This book is different. It will offer you inspiration, true stories, and basic steps. If you're looking for a book with detailed career information, please see the bibliography.

## Who should read this book?

This book is for you if you are contemplating or in the midst of a career transition. When you are going through any sort of change (career, marital, geographical, empty or new nest), it is very common not to know what you really want. Adults-in-transition classes are full of people who have spent years:

Doing for others

Being full time housewives/mothers
or househusbands/fathers

Taking the job that was offered at the time

Committing to their children's or their spouse's success

Taking care of elderly/ill parents

Being married (and are now divorced)

Many of these people have not taken the time to find out what they need to be fulfilled in their lives and careers. "I'm just not sure who I am anymore," is a common comment. If you can identify with being in transition, this book is for you.

This book is for you if you will be forced to make a career change due to:

Graduation from student to who-knows-what?

Company downsizing
A change in health
Physical injury
Retirement
Loss of spouse, or
Other life changes

For example, Joan was a successful restaurant manager who loved her work. When she suffered a back injury which severely limited her physical activities, and she could not stand on her feet for more than one hour at a time, restaurant management was no longer a career option for her.

Tom was a high ranking military officer. His duties in the service were clearly defined and he enjoyed his career. Now that he's retired, Tom is unsure whether he will be able to find employment that utilizes his military skills. He is not even sure if he wants to continue similar work, *if* a comparable job *were* available in the civilian market.

Situations like these can turn a confident individual into someone who feels empty, unfulfilled, and a little (or a lot) afraid. In these types of career changes you not only deal with the loss of an enjoyable career, you are also forced to figure out what you want to do next. The steps and stories in this book will help you make your next career choice. You may also want to consult a trained vocational rehabilitation and/or career counselor. Call the National Board of Certified Counselors at 1-910-547-0607 to locate a career counselor in your area.

## How to use this book

May this book be your companion. Read a few pages whenever you are concerned about your career. You are encouraged to keep a journal as you read. Every time you see this symbol, •J•, please do the journal writing exercise. This writing gives you a chance to listen to your inner voice, record, and review.

You will notice an abundance of quotes. Some of these quotes are from clients whose names have been kept confidential. Other quotes are from people who love their work, and there are also quotes that come from the Bible.

As one who grew up in a Christian home, studied at a Lutheran college and graduate school, and worked full time at a church before becoming a career counselor, I am aware of the comfort, guidance, and strength that can be gained from the Source of these verses.

Thank you to the contributors, those who love their work, and to those who are in the process of finding work they love. Enjoy reading and always feel free to send me your comments.

Sincerely,

Nancy Hanson, M.A.
President, Career Discovery
1441 Kapiolani Blvd. #2003
Honolulu, Hawaii  96814
March, 1995

# CHAPTER ONE

## You may need healing before you create work you love.

*"I know this job is for me."*

**After the second interview,**

*"Well, I thought it was for me,
and now I'm not so sure."*

**After the phone call,**

*"Hmm, I didn't get the job.
I wonder what was wrong with me."*

## CHAPTER ONE
### YOU MAY NEED HEALING BEFORE
### YOU CREATE WORK YOU LOVE.

What does healing have to do with creating work you love? Take the following test to see if you've been hurt in this hunt for enjoyable work. If you've been wounded, you just might need some healing.

**The wounded quiz**

1. Have you ever heard words like: "Thank you for applying; however, we have found someone else.
2. Have you ever applied for a job and come in number two?
3. Have you ever applied for a job and received no letter or phone call in response?
4. Do you ever feel as if your work under utilizes your gifts?
5. Have you ever been told that, even though you are the greatest employee, your position has been eliminated due to the bottom line?
6. Have you ever worked where several of your co-workers have been terminated and each day you wonder, "Hmm, when will it be me?"
7. Have you ever been one of those who was not laid off; therefore, doing the work of three people who were terminated?
8. Have you ever had a fantastic idea for starting your own business, and it didn't turn out exactly as planned?
9. When people ask, "...And what do you do for work?" do you ever cringe?
10. Are you afraid to leave your high stress job because you don't know what else you could do for work?

As you can see, there are lots of ways to feel trapped, worried, fearful, stressed, disappointed, hurt, cheated, rejected, used, failed, sad, tired, left out, discouraged, and down right bummed out. These feelings are wounds that need healing.

## Acknowledging the validity of your feelings

When consulting for Drake Beam Morin, Inc., an international outplacement firm, there's a phrase we use in the workshops, whether the group consists of high-level executives who are being "let go" after 25 years, or those who've worked only six months for a company.

The phrase is: "Acknowledging the validity of your feelings is crucial to your readiness for the next steps." If you are denying some of your feelings about yourself and your work, they may creep up on you at the strangest times. If you have open wounds and don't take some time for healing, you might bleed during your next interview! If you have no hurts, off to Chapter Two you go. If you do have a wound or two, welcome to the human race. Get some support and healing time under your belt. Then you will be ready for the next step and the next chapter.

## How hurt are you?

You're either a little hurt, a lot hurt, or somewhere in between. How much healing do you need? Probably a little, a lot, or some. You'll have more energy for creating enjoyable work when you've first paid some attention to any wounds you might have.

## What does healing mean, anyway?

Let's keep it simple. If you fell off your bike, you could have many different wounds. If you just skinned your knee, you'll feel stiff and probably stay off your bike for the rest of the day. On this same note, if you've had one interview and only one rejection, you can probably talk with a friend, have a good meal, take some deep breaths, say you didn't really want that job anyway, and continue looking as early as the

If you fall and get a deep cut, you'll feel stiff, get stitches, and maybe stay off your bike for a week or two. You may ask someone for help. Hopefully, you'll come home, put your feet up, and nurture yourself. You may not expect as much from yourself, because you are healing. You may stay home from an evening meeting and rent a movie instead. The wounded-from-work analogy here could be that you were told you have only four months left with a company you really like. Can you see how this could be a wound that needs healing? You're not losing blood; you're losing status, self esteem, and job security. You can say, "Oh, I'll be fine." Just remember that for most people, there are some feelings of loss that need to be expressed and healed. Take time to nurture yourself and heal when you get a wound.

Last on the continuum, you could fall, break a bone, and spend a night in the hospital. You may be told to stay off the bike for a month, use crutches, and stay in bed for a few days, to what? Rest! Recuperate! Heal! If you've been laid off, if you've been looking for work for several months, or years, chances are great that you are in need of some healing.

The purpose of this chapter is for you to identify any wounds you may have. Like it or not, in our culture, we get and give identity through our work. If your work has not been fulfilling, you may be carrying some hurt. Do what you would do if you were wounded from a bicycle fall. Decide how much time you need to stay off your bike. When you acknowledge your feelings and nurture your wounds, you're much better equipped to create work you love.

*Sometimes I think*
*I'm the luckiest person in the world.*
*There's nothing better than having*
*work you really care about.*

*Sometimes I think my greatest*
*problem is lack of confidence.*
*I'm scared, and I think that's healthy.*

**Jane Fonda**
*(acknowledging her feelings)*

# CHAPTER TWO

## LISTEN TO YOUR INNER VOICE TO CREATE WORK YOU LOVE.

*My advice is to live your life.*
*Allow that wonderful*
*inner intelligence*
*to speak through you ...*
*Follow your bliss and*
*be what you want to be.*

*Don't climb the ladder of success*
*only to find it's leaning*
*against the wrong wall.*

**Bernie Siegel, M.D.**
*Love, Medicine and Miracles*

## CHAPTER TWO
### LISTEN TO YOUR INNER VOICE.

You want to create work you love. Why not do as Martin Luther suggests: "Work as if everything depended on work; and pray as if everything depended on prayer."

If we define prayer as conversation, there is talking and there is listening. It may take some time before you actually sense this Spirit speaking to you. Invest the time in listening. Adding a spiritual component to your job search could be most rewarding.

If you are willing to consider the notion that there is a Being who wants the best for you and who unconditionally loves you, then this affects not only your career planning, it affects your life. Joel Goldsmith, the Christian mystic and author of over 30 books on spirituality calls this Being the "Infinite Invisible." Many call this Being God or Higher Power. In this book, this Being is sometimes called the Voice that is inside you.

In the profession of career counseling, there is a body of knowledge and skills that helps people in their search for meaningful work. This body of information has been translated for you into the steps you'll be reading about in the next few chapters. You will be asked many questions. To create work you love, listen to the still, small voice inside you ... that is the key. Buy a journal. Whenever you see this symbol •J•, you'll know it's time to write your answers. Acknowledge the Creator inside you, ask for guidance, then write.

## Ram's Story - Food for thought

Ram, a recent client, taught me about faith and the job hunt. He is originally from India and practices the Hindu religion. Although he admits he doesn't always live his belief, he believes all that really matters is being close and committed to God. That is all.

He has a spouse, three children, a Ph.D. in management from Purdue University, and was recently "downsized." Seeing me for career counseling was part of his outplacement package. I asked him what kind of work makes him the happiest. He said that whether or not he was "happy" in his job did not matter. Ram sees himself as a wave in the ocean, which, for him, symbolizes his oneness with the universe. He gets peace from the Creator of this universe as he lives out his "dharma" or duty to God, family, and friends. Getting happiness from his job did not compute.

There were parts of his upper level management position that Ram enjoyed, such as: solving problems, empowering co-workers, and receiving a salary that provided nicely for his family. He believes he would be reasonably satisfied selling vegetables on a corner.

For Ram, God is the only source of true happiness. The job title is immaterial. It is okay to have a good education and a high paying job, as long as he does not believe that these are what bring happiness. His certainty of belief was touching and challenging. This level of spirituality is perhaps deeper than many of us desire however; it is definitely food for thought.

## You In The Universe

The following meditation is helpful for anyone who may have a wounded self esteem. It was written for a weekend retreat called *You in the Universe*. Find a quiet place to read these thoughts. This meditation could be part of your healing.

*You In The Universe*

| Negative thoughts you may have: | Empowering affirmations you can choose: |
|---|---|
| I'm a nobody. | My Creator has gifted me with unique interests, values, and talents. There's no one else like me. |
| I am alone, separate, and lost. | The same Spirit that lives in me lives in all of us; therefore, I am connected to the world. |
| I am unloved, uncared for. | My Creator has an intimate involvement with me. I *am* loved and cared for. |
| I don't matter or count. | I *do* matter, count, and influence the world by who I am. I *can* make a difference. |
| I'm not worthy of self-exploration; therefore, I don't know myself. | Since I'm unique, it is my purpose to discover and develop my interests, values, and talents. |

*You In The Universe*

| Negative thoughts you may have: | Empowering affirmations you can choose: |
|---|---|
| To be loved and accepted I have to please others, and give up my uniqueness. | As I continue to love and accept myself, I am *more* loveable! |
| I am on the planet to survive, compete, and win. | I am on the planet to be in harmony with myself, others, and the Universe; and to use my gifts to contribute to the well being of all. |

*I am here today to let go, relax.*
*I listen to the Spirit within me.*
*I receive the answers that are inside me.*
*Thy will be done.*

*The Lord was not in the wind;*
*and after the wind,*
*an earthquake,*
*but the Lord was not*
*in the earthquake; and after*
*the earthquake a fire,*
*but the Lord was not*
*in the fire;*
*and after the fire,*
*a still small voice.*

**1 Kings 19:11b-12**

# CHAPTER THREE

You've got to believe you
can create work you love.

*You can choose beliefs
that limit you
or you can choose beliefs
that support you.*

**Tony Robbins**

## CHAPTER THREE
### BELIEVE YOU CAN.

Did you know that there are lots of people who love their work? For the last three years over 200 stories have been collected about such people. While reading these stories (my collection, plus reports from students), the following beliefs repeatedly surface:

**I can do anything**
**I never give up**
**I am grateful**
**Support is vital**
**I am solely responsible for my career growth**
**I take risks**
**I make a positive difference**
**I have always loved my work**
**Enjoyment is key**

What do these beliefs have to do with creating work you love? There is a popular school of thought that we are what we think. You've probably heard the Henry Ford quote: "Whether you believe you can or cannot, you are right."

To give you a feel for the variations of these beliefs, browse through the next pages. Use these phrases however you'd like. •J• Take out your journal and answer these questions: What beliefs do I already have? What beliefs would I like to adopt?

**In the words of those who love their work ...**

### I can do anything

I can do anything I want to do.

There is really nothing that I cannot do.

I grew up with the philosophy that I can do anything.

### I never give up

There's always a way.

I never give up the things I enjoy doing.

For me, challenging is fun.

When I hear no, that means just find another way to get what I want.

When people say no and reject my ideas, I am more inclined to stay with it.

I seem to thrive on the words, "It can't be done."

I am determined not to let anything or anyone keep me down for long.

I have a lot of perseverance.

When one thing didn't work out, I became an expert in another.

I have an intrinsic desire to succeed.

If I hang in there, I will eventually achieve something of great value.

I am determined.

### I am grateful

I am truly blessed.

There is always something to be grateful for.

Lucky me!

I was fortunate to discover my God-given talents early.

I am grateful that I love what I do.

## Support is vital

Without the support of family and friends,
I don't know if I could have made it.

It helps to have supportive people in my life.

Having a mentor helps me.

My spouse is 100% behind me.

My parents helped me, believed in me, and supported me.

I have had many mentors.

## I am solely responsible for my career growth

I take total responsibility for my life changes.

I grab every chance to learn from people.

I support my own career growth.

If I don't get off my butt, I could be stuck in a
meaningless job the rest of my life.

Personal conviction and a desire to excel help me
love my work.

I am a self-made woman/man.

I am my own mentor.

How much I enjoy or don't enjoy is entirely up to me.

It's my life.

It's what I make of it that matters, so I make the most
of it and enjoy.

## I take risks

It is necessary to visualize, take risks, and change.

My career growth is a direct reflection of how much
I've been willing to break through my fears and move
on when things got too comfortable or when I was
no longer learning.

My family supported risk taking and learning.

## I make a positive difference

Having an opportunity to make a positive impact on someone's life is key.

My favorite part about this lifestyle is the opportunity to make a difference.

I love my work because I make a positive difference in my students' lives.

## I have always loved my work

I enjoy all my job tasks.

I enjoy what I do.

I've always loved whatever I was doing.

I wouldn't change my job for anything.

I've enjoyed every job up to the point when I've learned and accomplished all that I could. Then I move on.

My work is natural for me. I am content and feel constant satisfaction.

There is no doubt in my mind that I am where I want to be.

I love all parts of my work.

## Enjoyment is key

I am the happiest when I follow my heart!

My work satisfies my soul.

Enjoyment is the most important thing about a career.

Enjoying my work is the key to success.

I love my job so much I don't think I'll ever quit.

There's got to be more to work than just money.

It doesn't matter what I do for work. What matters is how I am with it.

To enjoy my work, I have to first enjoy myself and my life in general.

No matter how much money I make, I will leave my job if I don't enjoy it!

I need to feel personal reward in my work.

Life is too short NOT to enjoy what I spend the better part of my waking hours doing. I make each day something to enjoy from the moment I wake to the time I close my eyes at night.

I do not focus on how much money I make.

I focus on whether or not I can get up in the morning and feel happy to be going to work!

## The basic steps in career development

In the first three chapters, you spent time on feeling, believing, and listening to the still, small voice within you. These actions will help you on this journey to create work you love. Now it is time to cover the basics of career development.

This is a relatively new field, with some of the pioneers (such as Donald Super and John Holland) still alive today. Almost all of the theories contain the following basic steps:

Gather self information (interests, values, skills, dreams, style, etc.)

Gather occupational information

Decide which occupation best matches you

Create an action plan

Balance work with the rest of your life

There's a lot more to career development than just acquiring skills. Granted, if you need a job tomorrow and use a placement agency to help you obtain employment, neither the agency or you have the luxury of looking at much more than your current skills.

You will probably do the best career planning when you're not looking for a job! Unfortunately, when you are gainfully employed, you're usually too busy to do future career planning. Be that as it may, when you follow these steps, you are taking charge of your own career. All the steps are here for you to create work you love.

# CHAPTER FOUR

## DISCOVER YOURSELF
## TO CREATE WORK YOU LOVE.

*Life ia a gift …*
*untie the ribbon and*
*enjoy the miracle*
*of your uniqueness.*

**Susan Luke**

*President*
*Luke Communications Group*

## CHAPTER FOUR
### DISCOVER YOURSELF.

### Humor in self discovery

Why did the song, *Don't Worry, Be Happy* become so popular? Perhaps it is because we loved being encouraged to relax and not worry. Please let this time of self discovery be a time to Not Worry and Be Happy. Olympic gold medal winner and skater Dan Jansen started winning when he stopped making it so important. Dan's sports psychologist, Dr. James Loehr, suggested including humor in his life on a daily basis. Loehr points out that children laugh 400 times a day on the average, compared with adults' 15 laughs. Humor relaxes the body and relieves stress. Enjoy this chapter on self discovery, okay?

### Gather self information

When you are unemployed or really unhappy in your current position, it is very tempting to bypass this step and jump right into looking for a job. If you feel you know yourself well, this step can be relatively short; and yet, it is still very important. Knowing who you are is the first step to knowing where you are going. Choose as many of the following self discovery exercises as necessary to help you gain a clear picture of who you are. •J• Get your journal and start writing.

## SELF DISCOVERY EXERCISE #1

### Write an article as if you already loved your work.

*There are several variations of this theme:*

You are on the cover of your favorite magazine.

A newspaper article features your successful career.

Your obituary is highlighted in your home
town newspaper.

What would the article say? What do you hope would be said about you? Choose one of the above. To be most effective, please take at least 30 minutes for this exercise. Put on your favorite music, maybe some classical baroque, like Pachelbel's Canon in D. To get good results, find a comfortable, quiet place to sit or lie. To get even better results, find someone to read the following to you while you are relaxing!

*Close your eyes. Take several big breaths in through your nose and out through your mouth. Relax your body starting with your toes, your feet, etc. Continue breathing and relax your whole body. Now, begin to imagine the scenario you have chosen. Your eyes are closed, your body is totally relaxed. Begin to fantasize in your mind's eye. (Let's use the example of being on the cover of your favorite magazine.) See the cover of the magazine. See YOUR name and face! Go to the page where your story begins. See another photo. Look at your face. See yourself happy, content, proud. Your story tells others how you got into the work you love. See yourself with all the confidence, money, education, wisdom, and guts you need to tell your story!*

*Open your eyes.* •J• *Get out the journal. Know that it could take some time to see yourself this way. Create more than one story. There are no wrong answers, no bad ideas. Just play. See your name, then a job title, then the story.*

| | |
|---|---|
| Barb Nakagawa: | Certified Public Accountant |
| Susan Brown: | Interior Designer |
| Sam Pearlman: | General Manager of the Ritz Carlton, Maui |
| Jack Jones: | Travel Journalist |
| YOUR NAME: | YOUR IDEAL JOB!! |

Be sure to include: what you like best about your work; what a typical day is like; your lifestyle; what your job environment looks like; how you got there; the obstacles you encountered and how you dealt with them; and advice you would give others. Congratulations! Each process is a piece of your puzzle. If you had no clue of what to write, try exercise #5B which is actually a variation of this exercise.

## SELF DISCOVERY EXERCISE #2

### Pretend you live on Pluto!

Let's say you moved to Pluto and were looking for work but didn't know what types of employment existed on the planet. The Pluto employment interviewer might say:

*"Since we have no comparable job titles with Earth, describe to me what you did on Earth. What part of your work did you like the best? What do you enjoy doing? Tell me about yourself, your interests, values, and skills. If you could do anything, what would it be? Here on Pluto, we have a system where everyone writes his/her own job description. Our productivity and morale are outstanding. Our employee retention and job satisfaction are quite high. We find this system works very well for us. Why don't you write down a brief job description for yourself, and I'll check back with you in a while."*

You may be dumbfounded. You may say, "Yeah, but, uhh ... may I see the job descriptions of the others first? I want to know what people are doing here on Pluto. Let me see what pays the best. At least tell me the current employment trends."

*"We don't do it that way on Pluto. We thoroughly researched Earth's method and it didn't seem to work very well. We are quite happy with our process here. Please, go ahead and write your own."*

•J• Get out the journal and write your own job description.

## SELF DISCOVERY EXERCISE #3

### What are your values?

What is most important for you in your ideal work? In their book, _Discover What You're Best At_, authors Barry and Linda Gale give a lot of attention to abilities. However, they also stress the importance of values. The Gales' comment, "Your value system determines your job satisfaction."

To help you identify what is important to you, here's a list of commonly held job-related values. Several of the values listed are taken from _Discover What You're Best At_. As you look them over, select the values that are most important for your overall job satisfaction. Feel free to add to the list. •J• Get out the journal, select, rank, and record your top values.

Accumulating large amounts of money.

Being in an environment that involves frequent change.

Being involved in work that contributes to the advancement of moral standards such as: spirituality, ecology, etc.

Belonging to an organization or group.

Coming up with new ideas in a creative way.

Enjoying my work.

Having day-to-day contact with the public.

Helping other people directly.

Performing a job that requires physical strength and stamina.

Performing similar tasks each day.

Receiving considerable recognition for my work.

Setting my own time schedule.

Taking extended vacations.

Taking risks as part of my work.

Traveling much of my working time.

Working as a member of a team.

Working primarily by myself.

Working where I can pursue the leisure activities
I enjoy most.

Working where there is an adequate salary.

Working where there is considerable security.

Working with definite deadlines.

Working where I will have opportunity to advance
in pay and responsibility.

Write your own.

## SELF DISCOVERY EXERCISE #4

### What about skills?

Are you wondering, "This interest and values stuff is nice but when do we talk about skills?" Of course, analyzing your skills is a vital part of self assessment. •J• Record in your journal your answers to these questions:

What are my current skills?

What skills do I most enjoy using?

What skills do I want to develop?

Am I willing to do what it takes to develop these skills?

## SELF DISCOVERY EXERCISE #5A

### The ideal job based on your Holland Code

The next exercise starts with identifying your Holland Code, which is derived from the six occupational themes created by Dr. John Holland. The Holland Code is currently the most widely used career planning tool and an excellent method of determining what occupational areas match you the best. Formal ways of determining your Holland Code include taking the Self Directed Search or the Strong Interest

Inventory. Consult a career counselor or college career center if you would like to take either of these. The Holland code consists of six personality types which are briefly described as: Realistic - dealing physically with the environment. Investigative - thinking, analyzing and/or problem solving. Artistic - creating, expressing, and/or designing. Social - counseling, teaching, and/or healing. Enterprising - leading, managing, and/or selling. Conventional - accounting and/or organizing. Choose which three words best describe you.

## Not Sure About Your Holland Code?

If you have difficulty deciding which types best describe you, know that it is not uncommon to be skilled in one area yet enjoy another. If you want to create work you love, you may need more training. If you see yourself as "trainable," then rule nothing out on the basis of skill. Here's a time when you might want to consult that "inner voice." Allow the spirit to guide you as you look at particular situations.

Analyze situations by the Holland Code. As an example, let's use a seminar hosted at a hotel. What parts of putting on this seminar are most attractive to you?

| Realistic: | arranging tables, chairs, transportation, logistics |
| Investigative: | researching the attendees; looking for any trends |
| Artistic: | creating the flyer, banner; selecting color, music, songs, poetry |
| Social: | welcoming, greeting, coaching, presenting, entertaining |
| Enterprising: | planning, figuring out how to make money |
| Conventional: | monitoring the registration; handling bookkeeping |

Usually you will feel attracted to one or two areas. You may even feel repulsed by an area. Listen to the voice within. The questions boil down to these: Who are you? What do you enjoy? What would you love especially if you could acquire more skills? To answer these, create quiet times of writing and listening. Look for themes and patterns in your likes.

## How do I know if I'd like to be a rock star if I've never been one?

Continue to explore career options through the Holland Code. Let's take rock star related careers for example:

| | |
|---|---|
| Realistic: | handling all the rigging of the rock concert |
| Investigative: | researching what lyrics sell best; conducting market research on album covers |
| Artistic: | creating the music; performing; entertaining |
| Social: | handling public relations with the fans, interviewers, etc. |
| Enterprising: | taking responsibility for marketing and selling the rock star |
| Conventional: | doing all the bookkeeping/ accounting |

What part would you like the best? At this point, do your best to select your top two or three Holland Codes. Then, get ready for Exercise 5B.

SELF DISCOVERY EXERCISE #5B

## Ideal Career Scenario

This exercise was introduced to me by Dr. Edward Colozzi, author of *Creating Careers With Confidence*. Similar to Exercise #1, you'll create your ideal career, this time using the Holland Code and your work-related values. Include what you do on a daily/weekly basis, the work setting, your co-workers, the geographical area in which you work, the clothes you wear, and how you look. Do you work alone, as a partner, or as a member of a team? Describe your lifestyle. Write down what you do in your work that is so valuable to others that you get paid $X per hour or month or year.

•J• Start writing in your journal.

## MY IDEAL CAREER

Your name and ideal career title, (could be a combination such as artist/plumber). Be sure to write in the present tense, for example:

"My Holland Code is Realistic, Artistic and Social. I enjoy doing realistic work such as carpentry and plumbing and spend two days per week on the average doing gardening and landscaping for a few select home owners. I enjoy the opportunity to select and create the most beautiful plants for their yards. I arrange flowers and bring them into these people's homes weekly. One day per week I teach floral arrangement classes."

Weave into your story your Holland Code and top values. You will start seeing a theme as you do these exercises. If this theme/pattern excites you, you are on the right track. With the enthusiasm you may also be feeling some self doubt. You may think, "Yeah, right. Why set myself up to be disappointed? This won't work for me!" These thoughts are natural, especially if your previous dreams and wishes have not come true. The main point of all these exercises is to help you clarify who you are and what kind of work would be the most satisfying for you.

## People who love their work

Bob Cherry always knew he loved the outdoors. Now Bob is a ranch manager and loves his work. Marcy Roberts loved organizing things since she was a child. Today, she is a professional organizer. Susanne Sims' deeply rooted value is to save Mother Earth! She now has a thriving business called Eco Logic. Jeff Fox loves playing the piano so much he would play even if he didn't make money! Read their stories. They created work they love out of their interests and values. You can too!

*I see work as life
and prefer to call it my lifestyle,
rather than my line of work.*

**Robert Cherry**

*Ranch Manager*

## ROBERT CHERRY, RANCH MANAGER

I grew up on a farm in Arizona so working outside with nature and animals has always come naturally for me. The first job I had was working as a mechanic, and I was not quite sure that I wanted this as a lifestyle for the rest of my days. I used my mechanical skills to get a job on a ranch, and after fixing several mechanical problems, I was asked to be the ranch manager. My favorite part of this lifestyle is the opportunity to make a difference. Building and improving the ranch property as well as improving the quality of life and health of the ranch animals are what I like most. I wouldn't really change anything about what I do here.

I love the sense of accomplishment with ranch improvement. We produce results you can see at the end of a project. The most challenging part of this work is creating a system that will generate income. I need to know how many cattle, goats, etc. I need to sell to make a profit.

One of my many mentors who happens to be one of my oldest friends, reinforces my ideals and goals, and maintains that there's probably nothing a person cannot do.

I see work as life, and prefer to call it my lifestyle rather than my line of work. If for some reason, I was in another line of work briefly, I'd look for a place like this ranch to spend my weekends. It's a lifestyle I enjoy. It suites me. I couldn't see myself sitting behind a desk all day.

I love my work because at the end of each day, I can see accomplishments. I try to do quality work I can be proud of. And, in the long run, it takes less time to build a straight fence than a crooked one!

*The gifts that we receive
from our mentors
come in all shapes and sizes —
time, patience, positive energy,
or a belief in you and your dreams.*

**Marcy L. Roberts, M.S.**
*Organizational Consultant*

## MARCY L. ROBERTS, M.S.
### ORGANIZATIONAL CONSULTANT

My current business started after having a 1988 Christmas party in my home. At this party, my friends and business associates saw how organized my home was and told me they would pay me to organize their homes and offices. Getting paid to do what I loved seemed too good to be true! It took only two clients with two different organizational needs to convince me that what I really wanted to do was viable. Observing how much my efforts were appreciated hooked me forever! In no time at all I was seeing clients in home offices, as well as downtown offices and businesses of all sizes.

I love all parts of my work which include both personal and professional organization. I have especially enjoyed setting up filing systems for individuals who are beginning their own businesses. It's been wonderful to help people get off to the right start – having a place for all the paperwork involved in beginning a business is essential! Of course it's always challenging to "rescue" those who have been in business but have let things get just a little out of hand – the "before" and "after" difference in just one appointment is extremely rewarding!

I remember asking my high school counselor what field I could study that would prepare me for a career where my natural organizational skills would be utilized to help others. I went on to get a Masters degree in Speech Pathology and worked as a Speech Pathologist for several years. I also wrote four children's workbooks designed to be used by parents for children ages 2-1/2 to 8 years old. My formal education was instrumental in training me to implement the "task dissection" theories of instruction. With these skills, I've been very successful at training others to set organizational priorities and goals in their businesses as well as teaching them how to maintain that organization on their own.

The hardest aspect of starting your own business is not knowing if there will be sufficient funds to pay your bills. My mentor, Jean Fitzgerald, believed in me. She knew that her active lifestyle would improve by utilizing many of my organizational skills. By becoming my first client, she gave me the opportunity to have a secure income from the beginning of my business, and this in turn gave me the financial freedom to establish a base clientele. What a wonderful gift – thank you Jean!

The gifts that we receive from our mentors come in all shapes and sizes – time, patience, positive energy or just a belief in you and your dreams. As each of you begin your business endeavors, don't forget to thank your mentors for their gifts to you.

*As each of you begin your
business endeavors, don't forget
to thank your mentors
for their gifts to you.*

**Marcy L. Roberts, M.S.**
*Organizational Consultant*

*Patricia Hayes once said to me:*

*"If you have connected with
a vision it is because you have
the ability to make it happen."*

*"The areas in which we are most deeply wounded
are our areas of greatest strength
and ability to teach, and show others the way."*

**Susanne Sims**
*Owner, Eco Logic*

## SUSANNE SIMS
## OWNER, ECO LOGIC

I found myself trapped in a smog inversion in Los Angeles. At that moment, I felt deeply hurt by the condition of our planet. Someone said to me, "The areas in which we are most deeply wounded are our areas of greatest strength and ability to teach and show others the way."

Even though I successfully sold advertising for six years, it did not satisfy my soul. I knew I would leave one day, but did not know for what. It took me about two years to define "what!"

The "what" is Eco Logic, an environmental communications company. My major job tasks include writing, speaking, recycling, consulting, and project work involving conferences. I know I am making a difference and I enjoy the freedom of being my own boss.

If I could change one thing it would be the attitude many have that environmental work should be free of charge and done by volunteers. I see myself as a pioneer in what will eventually become an industry. For now, I see my company's role as that of an educator – one which will bring forth action. I really haven't had a mentor. We are inventors, creating a whole new area of work. There is a great line that Patricia Hayes once said to me: "If you have connected with a vision it is because you have the ability to make it happen."

Don't be afraid to dream of the outrageous and to cast the highest vision! Always believe in the power behind what is motivating you.

When I started my company three years ago, I imagined myself working internationally but didn't know how that would come to pass. Today, I have clients in Geneva, Stockholm and Sydney, and I am traveling all over the world.

My next vision is to open The New Millennium Institute, an environmental retreat/learning center on the Big Island of Hawaii which is due to open in the spring of 1996. I now know that I am simply a conduit through which this project will manifest itself.

*I think that even if I didn't have to work
to make a living, I would still be doing
the type of work that I am doing now.*

**Jeff Fox**

*Professional Pianist*

## JEFF FOX
### PROFESSIONAL PIANIST

My occupational title is Pianist, specializing in private functions. I was asked by a very prominent family to perform at their Christmas party, having been referred by two respected people in the arts community. That first party got me started and the referrals started coming in from there.

I love playing the piano and having other people enjoy listening to my music; especially when I play their favorite piece. My favorite job task is creating the right atmosphere or mood for the function where I'm performing.

Before I started performing at special events, I taught piano privately for about five years until I stumbled into the performing side of the business. The most challenging part of my work is finding new clients. It's a difficult market to reach as the service I provide is what some might consider to be a luxury item. People don't have to hire my performance services the same way they don't have to buy a luxury automobile. That's why innovative marketing and creating a niche for myself are top priorities when it comes to securing bookings.

I've never really had a mentor, although I've been supported in the business sense by certain people in the community who truly appreciate what I do. They employ me a lot and continue to give me referrals. One event which had a great impact early on in my career was the opportunity to perform for one particularly well-known client. That performance gave me the credibility, exposure, and lots of "public relations" which was essential to expanding my client base.

# CHAPTER FIVE

## EXPLORE YOUR OPTIONS TO CREATE WORK YOU LOVE.

## CHAPTER FIVE
### EXPLORE YOUR OPTIONS
### TO CREATE WORK YOU LOVE.

You've spent some time on yourself. You've read about other people's jobs and their beliefs. "Yeah yeah yeah. What about me?" you could be wondering. You may be chomping at the bit to research your ideas.

*To create work you love, you've got to know your options, and know them well.* Occupational exploration is just as important as self exploration. The order in which you go through the process is the key. There is only one you to explore. There are over 12,000 occupations to explore, with new ones being created daily. Know yourself first, then your options automatically narrow. Remember all the time you spent creating your ideal job? That's the information you'll use to select the real world job titles that best match you! Your ideal job and your top values are your measuring sticks, your guiding lights.

Do you have to read thousands of job descriptions and measure each one with your guiding lights? No. There are better ways to find your options than paging through the entries in the Dictionary of Occupational Titles (DOT). You don't even have to grab the want ads and stare at each job listing. Thanks to career development researchers, career assessment designers, and labor market specialists, there are plenty of resources to utilize.

### Tools to help you narrow your options

The following tools can be found by consulting a career counselor. By identifying your **Holland Code** in Chapter Four, you automatically linked yourself with certain occupational areas. Holland's **Self Directed Search** provides job titles that best match you based on your code. The **COPSystem** is a series of three inventories which measure your skills, interests and work-related values. The system's combined results will recommend several occupational choices from fourteen career areas which best match your profile.

You may also choose to take the **Strong Interest Inventory** or the **Career Assessment Inventory**. These career planning tools match you with a Holland Code and related job titles based on your interests.

With these tools you can narrow the field from thousands to a handful of job titles. Use one or more of these assessment instruments to assist you in creating your list of five occupational options. An occupational card sort is a great tool to help you narrow your choices (see bibliography). When you have the titles that seem to match you best, you are ready to start researching.

When you're ready to research, the library and phone book should be your first sources of information because they are easily accessible and filled with information. Ask the reference librarian to show you the *Dictionary of Occupational Titles* (DOT), the *Guide for Occupational Exploration* (GOE), and the *Occupational Outlook Handbook* (OOH). You'll get occupational facts such as: job description, aptitudes needed, work setting, hiring practices, current employment, earnings, outlook, preparation, career ladder, and tips. The bibliography in this book lists sources of career information also.

*First Read,*

**Then Talk**

## First read, then talk

Let's assume you have five occupational titles you want to research. First read all you can about your options. Use the career reference section in the library. Read trade magazines. Read autobiographies. •J• Take notes in your journal. As you are researching, listen to your inner voice. Is it saying, "Yeah Yeah Yeah," or "No Way, Baby." Sometimes you'll love the job description, and can't live on the money. Or, you love the money, but after you read the job description, you don't think you could stand the job! Probably ditch that choice, unless money is your one and only job-related value.

Once you have researched the occupation, then talk to people who are doing it! Field interviews are not job interviews; they are meetings you schedule to learn more about an option you are considering. Make sure you know your stuff before you do your field interviews! Let's say you are interested in public relations and advertising, and you haven't researched the fields enough to know the difference between the two. You won't impress the professional you field interview if you haven't done your homework. Chances are even slimmer that he/she will ask you to volunteer or work part time or even take you seriously if you haven't taken the time to become knowledgeable about the field.

## To dos

•J• Store this information in a specific section of your journal. Use several pages for each job title and record your library research. Keep track of your personal friends and contacts in each field. Record names and the phone numbers you get from the phone book or other sources. Create a list of informed questions you plan to ask during your field interviews. Resolve to complete a specified number of tasks each week such as: call three businesses in the occupational areas in which you are interested to get more information. Visit the library every Thursday evening for two hours to research your options.

If it is at all possible for you, volunteer in your areas of interest. There is no better way to determine if an area is for you than to actually be in the environment! Sometimes the fringe benefits (like meeting great contacts) make volunteering definitely worth the time!

Sounds like a lot of work, eh? If you find a short cut to occupational research, let me know. One way to make this a bit shorter is to narrow your options to two or three. This is up to you. The main point here is that you need to research your options in order to make the best decision!

## How do I talk with people about their work?

You are not alone if you feel uncomfortable walking up to a stranger and saying, "Hi, you're doing what I think I want to be doing. Wanna talk?" Actually, talking with someone about work you've dreamed of could be fun.

Start by saying something like, "I'm in career transition. Your occupation is one of the top three that I am considering. I would love to spend 15-20 minutes with you to hear about your work and see your workplace. When would be a good time?" Buy them lunch. Volunteer for them. Listen. Share your enthusiasm.

## Be persistent in your occupational research

If at first you don't succeed, eat chocolate! Just kidding. The point of the following scenarios is that it might not always be easy to learn about your options. You've heard the phrase, "If it were easy, everyone would be doing it." You are reading this book to create work you love. To create work you love, you've got to know your options. To know your options you have to read first, then talk. Read the following scenarios, then start scheduling appointments with people who are in the kinds of work about which you want to learn more.

## Scenario #1.

You are interested in marine biology but don't know anyone in the field. There is no one in your area who does it. Use the library. Write a letter to an author or reference name (include a self addressed stamped envelope) and ask for more information or another resource person he or she could recommend. Take your next vacation to a place where you can meet professionals in marine biology. Visit a marine life park or a university that has a marine biology program. Call or write in advance; be persistent.

## Scenario #2.

You get the name of a marine biologist. You call her but she is too busy to speak with you personally and does not return your call. You consider giving up. What about writing her a letter? In your correspondence, you acknowledge her busy schedule, explain your interest in marine biology and your desire to explore the career field. Ask to visit the facility or for other professional contacts who may be of assistance to you. Offer to volunteer at the facility. Enclose a self addressed stamped envelope and information on how to contact you.

## Scenario #3.

You receive no response from the great letter you sent to Ms. Marine Biologist. That's OK, don't give up, just move on. Back to the library. Check out more books, new releases, current magazines. Are there new names, new phone numbers, other universities or related businesses you missed the first time?

## Best case scenario

Best case scenarios are a lot more fun to talk about! Let's say you want to be a principal of an elementary school. You talk with your son's principal. He says, "Sure, when would you like to come in?" Mr. Jones tells you about his training, what he wished he would have done differently, how he worked his way up to his current position. He then asks you if you would like to volunteer in his office, or be a teacher's aide at the school. So, with one phone call, you got a lot of valuable information, a personal contact in your field of interest, and the opportunity to work at the school to experience the work environment.

## Searching through the Want Ads

It is tempting to say "I don't know what jobs are out there; so, I have to look and see what I might want to do, or what I can do." That's a valid point; and doing this is likely to confuse you even more. Part of your anxiety about the newspaper could be because you haven't gotten clear on what you want. The rule of thumb for you to remember is ...

*Take one step at a time.*

*Searching for a job
before you have determined
what kind of job you want
is like putting the cart
before the horse!*

## One step at a time

Remember that creating work you love is a process with steps. If you follow these steps, your process will be much easier. When clients get laid off and opportunities for new jobs come quickly, sometimes they panic and ask me how to prepare for the interview. These outplacement clients receive a large notebook filled with tips for the job search, resume writing, interviewing, etc. etc. If they have time to review only one thing, I recommend they become clear on their "Ideal Job Preferences." This means, know what you want before you start looking for jobs.

Believe it or not, the same applies when you are car shopping. Do you know what happens if you enter a car dealership and have not taken the time to set your budget? What happens when you don't know what kind of car you want? You could accidentally find the perfect car; however, that's not too likely. If you don't take the time to establish your price range and your need for the car, you are quite apt to waste time and feel frustrated. Know what you want before you look for a job! How do you get to the place of knowing? Thoroughly know who you are (Chapter Four) and thoroughly research your options by reading and talking. Then, you're ready to look at the newspaper.

## Occupational research - The variety

You've just been encouraged to do occupational research, first by reading, then by talking with people. As you can imagine, there is such great variety in what you will learn. Ann and Joy are highlighted next to illustrate this variety. Ann always knew what she wanted. Joy has worked in over thirty different jobs. Both of these women love their work.

**I always wanted to be a nurse.**

You know those people, the kind that always knew what they wanted to be when they grew up. My mom's best friend knew she wanted to be a nurse when she was a little girl, and just finished her fortieth year of being a nurse. Your best friend always knew. Your older brother always knew. You could be thinking, "It's just not fair. How come I don't know?"

Ann has been a nurse for over thirty years. Now she is an administrator for a medical company that monitors women with high risk pregnancies. Ann has become a manager and salesperson. Her favorite part of the job is still, as it was in the beginning, making a difference in the patient's life. When she or a member of her staff gets a thank you letter filled with gratitude for the quality of care received, it makes it all worthwhile. It is possible to know what you want to do, do it, and love it all your life.

*My great grandfather was a judge.*
*My grandfather started the family law firm.*
*My mother and father are attorneys.*

**I want to be a chef.**

The other end of the spectrum from those who always knew what they wanted are those who have tried several different careers. Joy lives in Tampa, Florida and loves her work. She's had more than thirty jobs. Her current work is that of fashion consultant and her business card says "Professional-Know-It-All." The career paths for Ann and Joy are quite different. Enjoy reading their stories.

*The clinical work I do has been
my profession for 33 years. I loved it
when I started, I love it even more now.
It has changed and grown and so have I.*

**Ann Arnone**
*Nurse Administrator/Sales Manager*

## Ann Arnone
## Nurse Administrator/
## Sales Manager

My job as Nurse Administrator/Sales Manager was an outgrowth of a business venture I helped start in this community. It afforded me the unique opportunity to use 30 years of clinical nursing experience and expertise while learning business management.

Major corporate tasks I have learned include generating sales reports on a monthly basis, conducting performance reviews on all employees and handling marketing/sales responsibilities. My greatest job satisfaction comes from patient contact, clinical tasks, and watching the growth of the business.

The clinical work I do has been my profession for 33 years. I loved it when I started, I love it even more now. It has changed and grown and so have I.

The most challenging part of my work is spending so much time in a single office with women only. This often presents interpersonal problems. Empowering everyone to be their best and dealing with egos that sometimes don't blend is a constant management challenge.

My mentors were two peers who started as I did in the nursing profession and drew from their experience and natural talents to become very successful businesswomen in the healthcare field.

My career growth is supported by the company that employs me. They invest in my business education, give me the tools to do my job, and continue to challenge me to stretch.

*I have held over 30 different jobs including teacher, travel agent, manicurist, employment counselor, model, salesclerk, waitress, office manager, and even a clown at children's parties.*

**Joy Appleton**

*Professional Know-It-All*

## JOY APPLETON
## PROFESSIONAL KNOW-IT-ALL

My consulting work has grown out of a lifetime of experiences. I have held over 30 different jobs including teacher, travel agent, manicurist, employment counselor, model, salesclerk, waitress, office manager, and even a clown at children's parties.

As a self-employed Image Consultant, I help clients assess their appearance and wardrobe and assist them in focusing on the professional image they wish to project. In their homes, I advise them on closet organizing and sorting, coordinating new outfits, and forming a wardrobe plan. In addition, I take them shopping for outfits which, added to their present wardrobe, create their best professional look.

Although I also love speaking to groups, working with clients on an individual basis is my favorite task. The most challenging part of this work is getting clients to give up clothes that don't serve them.

Taking presentation courses most impacted my work. My instructor helped me see that I have many marketable talents that I previously took for granted.

If you are wondering how to get into this field, I suggest that you take classes and learn all you can about the world of grooming and fashion. The economy has not affected my work because people always need to look their best!

*The average American
entering the workforce today
will change careers - not jobs -
careers, three times,
according to the Labor Dept.
Private experts tell people to count
on five different careers.*

**Megatrends 2000**

*John Naisbitt & Patricia Aburdene*

# CHAPTER SIX

## CHOOSE TO CREATE
## WORK YOU LOVE.

*God, grant me the*
*SERENITY*
*to accept the things*
*I cannot change,*
*the COURAGE*
*to change the things I can*
*and the WISDOM*
*to know the difference!*

**The Serenity Prayer**
**Reinhold Niebuhr**

## Decision Making

*What do you want?*
*What does it cost?*
*What are you willing to pay?*

## CHAPTER SIX
CHOOSE TO CREATE WORK YOU LOVE.

Once you have narrowed your options to three to five job titles that best match your ideal job, you are ready to choose. A helpful decision making tool is the Decision Making Matrix by Dorothy Mitchell. The best way to illustrate this tool is to give you the example of someone we'll call Penny.

Penny used the checklist on pages 65-66 to determine her top priorities. In other words, what are the five most important things to you in work? Notice that "primarily working by myself" and "working as a member of a team" are both important to Penny. Hmmm. She described the work of a paralegal as one who does work on her own and at the same time works as a part of a team, the law firm.

**Penny's Top Five priorities for work:**
> Opportunity to be creative
> Primarily working by myself
> Working as a member of a team
> Adequate salary and security
> Enjoyment

**Penny's Top Four work options:**
> Paralegal
> Customer Service Representative
> Counselor
> Administrative Assistant*

*Penny includes Administrative Assistant to see whether **it is or is not** as bad a match for her as she thinks it is! This is where she has many of her current skills.*

Penny turns forty in a month and wonders, "Am I willing to pay the price of going to college for four to six years? Can I find work that I'll enjoy without a college degree?" We start with what Penny does know, her top five priorities and her top four career options.

**She followed these step by step instructions:**

1. List your top five priorities on far left column.
2. Rank these. 5 = high  1 = low.
3. Describe Top Five as simply as HI, MED, LOW, or with more detail.
4. List your top four work options on top of matrix on the right.
5. Take your first work option. In Penny's case, this is Customer Service Rep.
    a) On a scale of 1-5,
       Penny ranks the probable salary as a   "2"
    b) On a scale of 1-5,
       Penny ranks the enjoyment as a        "4"
    c) On a scale of 1-5,
       Penny ranks the creativity as a        "3"
    d) On a scale of 1-5,
       Penny ranks the working alone as a    "3"
    e) On a scale of 1-5,
       Penny ranks the teamwork as a         "5"
6. Still with Customer Service Rep
    a) On Salary multiply the "2" with the Rank Rating of 4 to get "8"
    b) On Enjoyment multiply the "4" with the Rank Rating of 5 to get "20"
    c) On Creativity multiply the "3" with the Rank Rating of 2 to get "6"
    d) On Alone multiply the "3" with the Rank Rating of 3 to get "9"
    e) On Teamwork multiply the "5" with the Rank Rating of 1 to get "5"

## PENNY'S DECISION MAKING USING TOP FIVE
## DECISION: WHAT WORK WILL BEST MATCH MY TOP FIVE?

| Top Five | Rank Rating | Description of Top Five | Customer Service Rep | Master's Degree Counselor | Admin. Asst. | Para-legal |
|---|---|---|---|---|---|---|
| Adequate Salary | 4 | 5 $40,000 per yr. or more<br>3 $30,000 per yr.<br>1 $20,000 per yr. or less | 8 / 2 | 12 / 3 | 12 / 3 | 12 / 3 |
| Enjoyment | 5 | 5 I enjoy work 75% of the time or more<br>3 I enjoy work 50% of the time<br>1 I enjoy work 25% of the time or less | 20 / 4 | 25 / 5 | 5 / 1 | 20 / 4 |
| Opportunity to be creative | 2 | 5 I am creative at least 50% of the time<br>3 I am creative 25% of the time<br>1 I never get to be creative | 6 / 3 | 10 / 5 | 4 / 2 | 8 / 4 |
| Opportunity to work alone | 3 | 5 I work alone at least 2/3 of the time<br>3 I work alone 1/3 of the time<br>1 I am with people all the time | 9 / 3 | 9 / 3 | 15 / 5 | 9 / 3 |
| Opportunity to work with a team | 1 | 5 Team-work based company<br>3 Each person for herself company<br>1 Always work alone, no team | 5 / 5 | 5 / 5 | 4 / 4 | 5 / 5 |
| **TOTALS** | | | 48 | 61 | 40 | 54 |

Above model adapted from Dorothy Mitchell,
*The Art of Helping*, Windward Community College, Kaneohe, Hawaii

7. Customer Service Rep gets a total of 48 points.
8. Follow steps 5 and 6 for each work option.
Then compare.

The next exercise gives you a chance to assess your "Top Five." •J• Get your journal, ruler, and complete your own matrix. If you get confused, refer to Penny's example.

## Career decision making steps before matrix

This worksheet prepares you for your matrix.

1. Identify the decision. For example:
What occupation will best match me?
2. Gather all self information:
(Holland Code, values, skills, etc.).

For TODAY, select your TOP FIVE priorities regarding work from the following list:

Opportunity to be creative: ARTISTIC

Opportunity to use my hands/be physical with environment: REALISTIC

Opportunity to analyze, problem solve: INVESTIGATIVE

Opportunity to work with people in a helping, caring way: SOCIAL

Opportunity to lead, manage or sell: ENTERPRISING

Opportunity to sort, organize, work with numbers: CONVENTIONAL

Earning adequate salary and considerable security

Setting my own time schedule

Being in an environment that involves frequent change

Performing similar tasks each day

Traveling much or at least some of my working time

Working primarily by myself

Enjoyment

Opportunity for advancement

Opportunity to work alone

Location

You may add others.

3. Of your top five, rank the top one a "5", next highest a "4", and so on.

4. List four career options. Keep your current position as one option, if it is.

5. •J• Create your own decision-making matrix in your journal.

Which option best matches your TOP FIVE priorities? What information do you need to better decide?

## The value of the matrix

Believe it or not, the total number of points any one career option receives is probably not the most valuable part of the exercise. Obviously, the higher the number, the more the option matches you. What is not so obvious is how you feel about your final scores: Assured? Relieved? Disappointed?

You could be saying, "Oh shucks! I wish entrepreneur would have gotten more points!" If this happens, re-examine the ranking of your Top Five. Are adequate salary and security really your top priorities? As an entrepreneur, there is a chance you could make lots of money. There is also a possibility you could go in the hole. If risk taking was your top value this would be an easier decision.

Sometimes your matrix reminds you that you don't know enough about your options. In this case, list the questions that come up, such as: How much money would I make? Would I enjoy it? Do more research and field interviews. If possible, spend one or more days with someone who is doing what you would like to do. In other words, go back to researching your options.

### The grass is greener in any other job
### Maybe so, maybe not!

Sometimes people think almost anything would be better than their current work situation. They do this matrix and discover: "No wonder I am so unhappy! My current job matches almost none of my Top Five. Yikes!" By doing the matrix, Penny discovered that Administrative Assistant, in fact, did not match her very well. Other times people find out that, "Huh! My job matches me more than I realized. I guess it is not that bad."

### Kinds of decision making

You have just looked at a planful approach to decision making. Listening to your inner voice could be called intuitive decision making which will give you great insight as to what option matches you best. Actually, combining planful with intuitive decision making is combining the best of both methods. The methods to avoid are impulsive, delaying, and compliant (letting someone else decide for you). It is your career and your decision.

### Starting your own business

You may have noticed that some of the people high-lighted in this book own their own businesses. If this is one of your options, be sure to make use of the many resources available such as the Small Business Administration, the Chamber of Commerce, and of course, the library. Do your homework before deciding.

## Getting more training

You may be considering a career option that calls for more training. Read the stories of Lynette, Zella, and Cynthia in Chapter Seven. They achieved their educational goals against the odds and will be a great inspiration for you.

## What did you decide?

Have you chosen the career that best matches you? If so, move on to the next chapter. If not, consider the following:

Spend more time gathering self and occupational information

Check out a helpful book (see Bibliography)

Pray/meditate/listen to inner voice

Talk with a supportive friend

See a counselor

Take a walk or bubble bath

# CHAPTER SEVEN

## PLAN TO CREATE
## WORK YOU LOVE.

*If you don't know where you
are going, you may end up
somewhere else.*

**David Campbell**

## CHAPTER SEVEN
### PLAN TO CREATE WORK YOU LOVE.

Once you have chosen a career that best matches you, the next step is to create a plan. It may take five or more years to achieve your career goal. How do you stay focused? How do you get there?

### Read your story daily

Remember your guiding light, your ideal job scenario that you wrote in Chapter Four? What if it was a ten (on a scale of one to ten with ten being GREAT!) when you started and now, it looks like a seven? That's OK, just don't give up! Why has it dropped to a seven? What's missing? Review, refine, rewrite. When you can identify what is missing, you are clarifying what you really want and need in your ideal work.

Do you feel as if your dream is too big? Do you get discouraged rather than excited? You always have options. You could quit the process all together. Decide it is hopeless. Or, rewrite your ideal job with enough reality so that you truly can see yourself doing it. You can always add to it later. Before you write your action plan, you need to have a future goal that you are excited about. Rewrite an exciting ideal, yet realistic, job. While you write, be sure to consult the still, quiet voice within. Ask for guidance, then write. Vow to read this daily. Reread Susanne's story on p.40 for inspiration.

### What next?

Determine approximately how long it will take you to get to this ideal job: Ten years? Five years? Two years? Six months? Hopefully, your ideal job will be so exciting and powerful that you will be ready and willing to take those sometimes difficult steps needed to get there. In his book, *How To Get Out of Debt, Stay Out of Debt, and Live Prosperously,* Jerrold Mundis lists some examples of goal setting. Let's look at the goal of being a talk show host:

| | |
|---|---|
| Five year goal: | Be a talk show host. |
| Three year goal: | Be a guest host for a radio show and a local TV show. |
| One year goal: | Be familiar with the range of possibilities for being a talk show host, from local radio to network television. |
| Six month goal: | Volunteer at both a radio and television talk show in any capacity. Research and learn. |
| One month goal: | Know roughly how many talk shows are available on television and radio in the area and what they are like. |
| One week goal: | Check one day's radio listing, marking with a highlight pen all the talk shows offered. |

## Now it is your turn!

•J• Take out your journal and write your five, three, and one year goals, as well as one month and one week goals.

## Goals: You are the boss

Who writes the goals? YOU do! Who is in charge: The goals or you? YOU are, of course. If you don't reach one of your goals in your original time frame what do you do?

Beat yourself up?

Feel guilty and give up?

Rewrite the goal?

Hmmm. Tough choice, eh?

## Three keys in goal setting

**KEY #1. Create goals to SERVE you,
not to produce worry or guilt.**

Rewriting goals is great! Achieving four out of five goals is great! You establish goals to help and to serve you.

**KEY #2. Write goals that are within your control
for example:**

Get advice on how to improve my resume

Rewrite my resume

Conduct library research on five companies

Write five networking/cover letters

Mail five resumes with cover letters

Make follow-up calls to the five businesses

All of the above steps are absolutely within your control. Getting the job is not within your control. You can't make an employer hire you. You can control your steps to secure employment with an attractive company, such as having a dynamite resume, being prepared for the job interview, and obtaining the appropriate training or education which qualifies you for the job. Invest your time and energy on things you can control!

**KEY #3. There is magic in action!**

If you take small, measurable steps toward your goal, you will eventually get positive results. Let's say you have a goal to field interview ten people who are in occupations that are attractive to you. The results could look like this:

| Meeting #1 | The person was not interested in meeting with you. |
| Meeting #2 | You showed up, she forgot! |
| Meeting #3 | You met and felt like it was a waste of time. |
| Meeting #4 | You met, really enjoyed the person and information. |
| Meeting #5 | This person gave you names of two people you really need to know! |
| Meeting #6 | You were asked to volunteer for his company! |
| Meeting #7 | As a volunteer, you had lunch with a great contact. She introduced you to a person who needs to hire someone like YOU! |
| Meeting #8 | You casually met with this person and told her your ideal job scenario. |
| Meeting #9 | You had an official job interview. |
| Meeting #10 | You were offered the job! |

What if you gave up after the first three interviews? There is magic in action. Harvey Mackay, author of three best selling books, including the excellent career planning book, *Sharkproof: Get The Job You Want, Keep The Job You Love ... In Today's Frenzied Job Market* sent me the following story.

### ANYTIME YOU FEEL LIKE QUITTING
(author unknown)

He failed in business in '31.

He ran as a state legislator and lost in '32.

He tried business again in '33 and failed again.

His sweetheart died in '35.

He had a nervous breakdown in '36.

He ran for state elector in '40 after he regained his health.

He was defeated for Congress in '43,

He was defeated again for Congress in '48.

He was defeated when he ran for the Senate in '55.

He was defeated for U.S. Vice Presidency in '56.

He ran for the Senate again in '58 and lost.

This man never quit.

He kept on trying till the last.

**In 1860 this man, Abraham Lincoln, was elected President of the United States.**

Throughout your career planning journey, remember this story.

## Success against the odds ...

Lynette worked as an assistant manager for a fast food restaurant while raising her five children as a single mother. She had many reasons why it would be difficult to pursue her dream. However, sick and tired of being poor, she decided that seeking a higher education would be the best way to qualify for more interesting, higher-paying employment. Lynette had not been to school in over twenty years. She took the plunge and enrolled in a couple of classes at a community college.

Lynette had no money for school expenses or child care, and no spouse to assist her with the children while she attended classes. She made use of the resources she had and asked family and friends for help. She researched scholarships and tuition assistance at the local library. On a borrowed typewriter, Lynette completed several applications for scholarships offered by sources ranging from Clairol to Orville Redenbacher. She received financial assistance and eventually completed her bachelor's degree. There's more.

Lynette worked full time while taking the college courses and raising her family. She states "I know my family may have suffered, but I was suffering, too. I knew they would get the short end of the trade off if I didn't go for something that would make me happy and eventually make me a much better parent." At this writing, Lynette has completed her master's degree and is very close to getting her doctorate. She had almost every strike against her, every reason not to do it, and SHE IS DOING IT!

After you read Lynette's story, you will read about Zella who grew up in a Detroit ghetto. Through having a plan, believing in herself and in a power greater than herself, she became successful in corporate America. She now owns a profitable business with her husband and loves the freedom of being able to spend quality time with her family. You will also read about Cynthia who decided to apply to medical school at age thirty-six. Today she is a practicing physician. These women succeeded against the odds by having a plan. You can too.

## DR. CYNTHIA BURDGE
## PHYSICIAN

I was a medical technologist specializing in blood banking for fourteen years. I reached a point where I felt I had done this job "to death." I knew I could not continue indefinitely. By chance, I had the occasion to use specialized donor techniques therapeutically on very ill patients and found I could cope well in that environment.

Due to my desire to change jobs, I considered switching to forensic pathology upon being encouraged by a pathologist. I realized I would want to do that only if I went in as a physician, so at age thirty-six, after two years of preparation, I went to medical school.

My major emphasis is preventative care which includes screening for cancer, and for heart disease, and controlling of chronic problems. My favorite part of this practice is designing a therapeutic regimen for a patient which causes minimal side effects, is easy to live with, and is as inexpensive as possible. I have experienced the joy of seeing a patient's lifestyle improve after implementing some of my recommendations. Those patients are doing better and feeling better than they have in a very long time.

Any job has elements you may not enjoy, so you have to look at the overall value of the job. Even if it's just for a paycheck, your job can allow you time to develop your skills and plan ahead for the type of work that would please you more. If I had not been dissatisfied being a lab technician, I might not have moved on to becoming a doctor. I was able to develop some new skills and find a profession that pleases me.

Something that has had a great impact on my career was the growing realization that I could do more than I had previously thought. I could greatly increase my level of accomplishment as long as I was willing to take some considerable risks.

*Having an opportunity to make
a positive impact on someone's life
is what I love about my job.*

**Lynette Cruz**

*West Oʻahu Coordinator
Angel Network Charities, Inc.
Lynette and her daughter*

LYNETTE CRUZ
WEST O'AHU COORDINATOR
ANGEL NETWORK CHARITIES, INC.

I was an advocate for the homeless at Sand Island Beach on O'ahu. My sister and her children lived on the beach when the state tried to have campers removed. I helped them organize and resist.

I was asked to be the Executive Director of East O'ahu Housing Corp. and help homeless families find housing through the state program in 1990. In 1992, I went to work for Angel Network. It was then that I became aware that there were so many homeless families who were Hawaiian.

I was hired by the Network to do grant writing and I also volunteer as a case manager. I work two jobs simultaneously. Both jobs give me the flexibility to work my own hours. The best thing about this arrangement is that I can efficiently use my time working any hour of the day and night. My Hui Na'auao job as sovereignty education instructor ties in with my work with the homeless Hawaiians.

What I want to change about my work is that I would like to eliminate all the power struggles. In both jobs, I find that people continually engage in power plays in an effort to control the situation. This behavior interferes with positive relationships and working environments. Those people keep the team from developing as individuals and as a group.

Before I pursued this, I taught a college-level course, "Introduction to Cultural Anthropology". I was also a land-use history writer. Neither of these jobs gave me the satisfaction I have now. Having an opportunity to make a positive impact on someone's life is what I love about my job.

The most challenging part of my job is working with people. People are unpredictable. It's sometimes easier to deal with people when you keep them at a distance. This job keeps me face to face with people in problematic situations. I keep a good relationship with others and at the same time, try to help them solve their problems. That's very challenging and I like the challenge. I do not forget that the people I work with are human beings just like myself.

One of my mentors was my advisor at college. He told me that one day I would be "fired up" to do something. I waited for that moment. Being on the beach and seeing Hawaiians, young and old, struggling just to make a living "fired" me up to do something to help them. It was the turning point for me.

My children support me in many ways including encouraging me to continue schooling. They helped me take care of their younger siblings. My youngest son was born during my first semester of college.

I was a single parent with five young children when I started college. It had been almost twenty years since I had been to high school. With the support of my family, I graduated with a bachelor's degree in Pacific Studies from Hawaii Loa College. I went on to the University of Hawaii and received a master's degree in Anthropology. I am currently working on my doctorate degree with only the comprehensive exams and dissertation left to complete.

I am re-married now and am grateful to say that my husband always stands behind and beside me when I need support.

"I have a sense of greatness
which comes from feeling that
I'm doing what I'm supposed
to be doing on the planet —
empowering people,
especially women.

I am a woman in progress.
I'm just trying, like everyone else.
I try to take every conflict,
every experience, and learn from it.
All I know is that I can't be anybody else.
And it's taken me a long time
to realize that."

**Oprah Winfrey**
*Ladies' Home Journal*
February, 1994

*I surround myself with
supportive and positive people
(spouse, business partners, employees).
I nurture my faith in God
and try to remain thankful for
everything positive in my life.*

**Zella Jackson**

*Professional Speaker, Consultant, & Author*

## ZELLA JACKSON
### PROFESSIONAL SPEAKER, CONSULTANT & AUTHOR

I was fortunate to discover my God-given talents early and had the opportunity to develop my skills in these areas. During my freshman year in college I donated my time to causes that thrust me into the limelight (encouraging women and ethnic minorities to pursue technical careers). I gave speeches, chaired committees, etc.

Today I design and conduct educational programs on a commercial basis. Since 1981, I have provided classroom training, consultation and task force sessions with business owners and their key marketing and sales staff throughout the mainland U.S. and the Hawaiian Islands. Starting in 1991, I concentrated more on my writing, which has afforded me more time with my family. In fact, my professionally-produced video training program provides my long distance clients a valuable educational experience.

I have a mechanical engineering degree with an MBA. I worked for years in technical areas. My primary motivation was to gain valuable corporate experience so my "love" could be more easily pursued. As it turns out, engineering proved a great foundation and allowed me to springboard into what I currently do.

I've had three mentors: my husband, a dear friend, and Oprah Winfrey. Oprah is an inspiration and role model. Talk about beating the odds! In addition, my boss at Lansing's Board of Water & Light was the most supportive person I have ever worked for. Lastly, my calculus teacher in Jr. High school was instrumental in getting me accepted at an elite school where the question was, "What college are *you* going to?" – NOT – "Are you going to college?"

*No one can arrive*
*from being talented alone.*

*God gives talent,*
*work transforms talent*
*into genius.*

**Anna Pavlova**

# CHAPTER EIGHT

### Balance career with personal life to create work you love.

*Be gentle with yourself.*
*Nurturing yourself with unconditional love,*
*listening to your body, and rewarding*
*yourself with frequent celebrations can put you*
*in touch with your inner passion and power.*
*Most Americans try to high-pressure*
*themselves into higher performance.*
*Instead, be gentle and trust yourself*
*to find your own way.*

**Ann McGee-Cooper**
*You Don't Have To Go Home*
*From Work Exhausted*

*Fatigue makes cowards of us all.*

**Vince Lombardi**

## CHAPTER EIGHT
### BALANCING CAREER WITH LIFE.

Most of us grew up with a simple definition of career: Career is work. Career theorists are now saying that career equals work plus play. In her book, *You Don't Have To Go Home From Work Exhausted,* Ann McGee-Cooper suggests we are better workers when we add play to our lifestyle! Donald Super defines career as the sum total of the time and energy you spend in *all the roles* you play. As part of your career planning you need to answer the question, "How will my work fit into my life?"

How can you balance work with personal and family life? Listed below are five keys to help you.

Define your personal VISION of balance.

Decide what you need to ADD.

Decide what you need to SUBTRACT.

Start this week with one doable, enjoyable, measurable ACTION.

Find a SUPPORT PERSON to help, coach, and encourage you.

### Define your personal VISION of balance.

What does a balanced life look like to you? Use the Career Rainbow and Balance Wheel on pages 89-90 to guide you. Reread your ideal career scenario which includes your lifestyle. Then, boil it down to one sentence. Sam Horn, President of Action Seminars, and a person who loves her work, has one sentence that guides her:

*"My purpose is to make a
positive difference for as many people
as possible while maintaining a happy,
healthy lifestyle with friends and family."*

**Sam Horn**

In his book, *The Seven Habits of Highly Effective People*, Stephen Covey encourages every person to create such a "mission statement."

Complete the following two sentences in your •J• journal. "A balanced life for me looks like ..." and "My purpose statement, my guiding light, that helps me say yes and helps me say no is ..."

## How to best use the Career Rainbow and Balance Wheel

First of all, take LOTS of time to acknowledge yourself for the areas in which you feel satisfaction. This is important. After you have patted yourself on the back, then choose the area you want to change. You may be most unsatisfied with your "worker" role. Choose actions to help you start creating work you love. Does this mean that you ignore all of the other areas? No. Setting a priority means, "I will spend time on this first." While you are planning a career change, it may not be the best time to train for a marathon; however, you could fit in three hours per week of walking or aerobic dancing. And, you may be a better career planner for doing so!

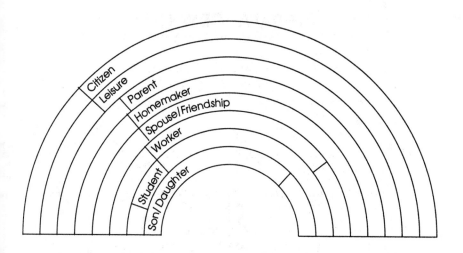

## THE CAREER RAINBOW (Adapted from Donald Super)

**CITIZEN-** Volunteering in community, church, civic & political areas.
**LESURITE-** Engaging in activities for relaxation, such as tennis, TV, etc.
**PARENT/GRANDPARENT-** Rearing, supporting and/or being with children.
**HOMEMAKER-** Managing a home through cooking, cleaning, etc.
**SPOUSE/FRIEND-** Building and maintaining a close relationship.
**WORKER-** Participating in part or full time paid employment.
**LEARNER-** Gaining knowledge/skills through reading or coursework.
**SON/DAUGHTER (OR CAREGIVER)-** Caring for parents or other relatives.

The rainbow bands I am satisfied with: _____

One rainbow band I want to change: _____

One action I will take this week to change this band: _____

_____

I ask_____to support me by _____

**EXAMPLE:**  **I want to change my leisure band.**
**I'll go to the beach for at least one hour this week.**
**I'll ask Tom to support me by joining me.**

# THE BALANCE WHEEL
## (source unknown)

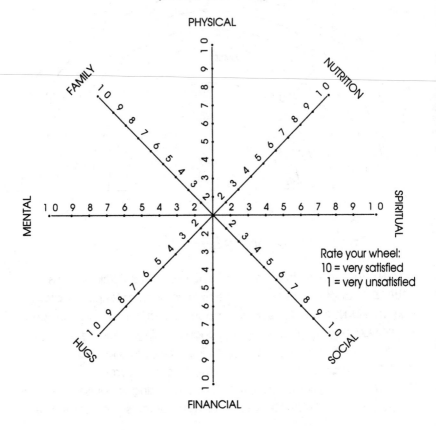

Rate your wheel:
10 = very satisfied
1 = very unsatisfied

The spokes in my wheel I am satisfied with: _____

One spoke I want to change:_____

One action I will take this week to change this spoke: _____

_____

I ask_____to support me by _____

**EXAMPLE:** **I want to improve my spiritual life.**
**I'll attend a church/worship service.**
**I'll ask Lyla to support me by going with me.**

## What if you are unsatisfied with many areas?

Reread your personal vision of your balanced life. Ask yourself to prioritize. Even while managing multiple priorities, you still need to decide, "What shall I focus on first?" When a former client assessed her rainbow, it became clear that getting at least one good friend was her first priority. She felt lonely and wanted a new friend more than a job change. Realizing this, she took some pressure off herself about finding a better job. Creating a new friendship was her priority. On any given day, if she had time for only one task, she would use that time for her friendship goal. She still planned on looking for more rewarding work, but this was a secondary goal.

Another client indicated that he was not satisfied with his relationship with his mother; however, finishing his college degree was his number one priority. He consciously chose to put the relationship with mom on the back burner. He stated, "I do want to get along better with mom. Now is just not the time. My education is more important. If I have time and energy left, I may work on our relationship; but finishing school is my top priority."

In your heart of hearts, what area is your number one priority? What is number two and number three? Choose to work on these in that order. Leave the rest for later.

## Decide what you need to ADD.

Many people often put themselves last on their priority list. You've heard it before: How can you be of any use to others when you haven't taken care of yourself? Perhaps you will choose to ADD doing one field interview each week. This is an action *for you* which will help you in your process of creating work you love. Or, you may choose to volunteer two hours per week with an organization for which you would love to work.

Some people want to add a spiritual dimension, like meditating and/or praying daily for five minutes. Using both charts, select the one area that is most lacking for you. What is one measurable, doable action you'd enjoy ADDING? Tell your support person and ask for encouragement.

Examples of actions to ADD:

I will choose an agency and volunteer
two hours per week.

I will buy my favorite magazine, soak in the tub,
and read!

Our family will eat one dinner together once a week.

## Decide what you need to SUBTRACT.

For many people this is the most important step, and perhaps the most difficult. Are you thinking, "I have just got to quit working these long hours! And, I don't know how!" Creatively brainstorm with a supportive friend. Discuss your decision to work fewer hours per week with your boss. Believe that it is possible. Check out a time management book at the library or take a time management class.

Sometimes you need to subtract volunteer hours. There are perhaps a few people who have too much leisure and choose to cut down on that! Use both charts to determine the one area you feel is taking too much of your precious time. What is the one measurable, doable action you will take that will allow you to SUBTRACT?

Examples of actions that will help you SUBTRACT:

I give the boss five suggestions on how
to reduce my work load.

I take the bus so I can read and meditate
rather than drive to work.

I say no to teaching Sunday School this year.

## Can you have it all?

When you are planning your balanced life, be careful who you use as a model. You may be setting yourself up for disappointment if you have the unrealistic expectation of being like certain actors on TV or models in magazines:

They are thin and gorgeous.

Their homes are beautifully decorated and always clean.

Their kids seem to always get along.

Spouses are always happy with each other.

Everyone has rewarding work.

Are you trying to be the fit, pleasant, organized, clean, Super Parent/Spouse that Ward or June Cleaver was?

A workshop participant made the comment, "I believe we can have it all, just not all at once!" Realize that it takes time. Living a balanced life is definitely a process. Use the charts as tools to assist you in setting your priorities. Choose action steps you will enjoy doing.

# CHAPTER NINE

## PEOPLE WHO LOVE THEIR WORK GIVE ADVICE.

*I really feel blessed
in so many ways,
because I've had the chance
to take this amazing journey.*

*Like everyone else,
my life has been shaped by
challenge and disappointment.*

*But what I've learned is
when you trust your instincts
and follow your heart
dreams do come true.*

**Michael Bolton**

*This is Michael Bolton - video*

# CHAPTER NINE
## PEOPLE WHO LOVE THEIR WORK GIVE ADVICE.

What do the following have in common: feeding hogs at 5:00 a.m. in the bitter cold; being a single parent trying to provide for one's children; weighing over 300 pounds; and not being very good at public speaking? Each of these four situations could be described as rather discouraging. Each person who had these situations now loves his/her work: oceanography, world traveling, weight-loss consulting, and presentation coaching, respectively. You'll read their stories at the end of this chapter.

As mentioned in Chapter Three, over the last three years, more than 200 stories have been collected about people who love their work. A few of the questions they responded to were: "Have you ever felt discouraged and/or felt like quitting? If so, how did you get help? What advice would you give someone who doesn't think it is possible to enjoy work?"

If you are a member of the human race, you've probably had at least a bit of discouragement in your career path. Following are answers to these questions. Turn to this chapter whenever a wave of discouragement comes your way.

*Watch for big problems.*
*They disguise big opportunities.*

**Life's Little Instruction Book**

**Have you ever felt discouraged and/or felt like quitting? If so, how did you get help?**

Here are some responses from people who love what they do.

At times I have been overwhelmed by my workload and have had trouble coping. I have consulted a psychiatrist from time to time and this has helped relieve the stress of my occupation.

I remember when I was still in the lab, trying to decide if I could handle the risk of medical school at my advanced age. My mentor gave me a realistic view of the problems in the medical profession. He also gave me proof that these problems could be surmounted. He told me I had the ability to be a doctor if I was willing to work for it, and gave me the encouragement I needed when my doubts were getting the best of me.

Dr. Cynthia Burdge
*Physician*


Sure, I've felt discouraged from time to time over the past nine years, especially in the beginning. There was so much to be improved, water supply, fencing, buildings, etc., etc. I deal with discouragement by identifying the "worst" task I have to accomplish. On any given day, I pick the one project I dread the most and schedule it as the first thing to be taken care of. Oftentimes, the actual work is not as bad as thinking about it!

I also do my best to change what might seem like a bad situation into something manageable by turning it around. The bigger the challenge, the better I feel when I've met or handled it! I look at the positive side of things and try to focus on the results of my efforts.

Robert Cherry
*Ranch Manager*

I went through periods where I didn't have any bookings at all and became discouraged. I realized I had to do something to create an interest in my profession, and began thinking of a number of unusual ways in which I could market myself. I started donating performances to charity functions, advertising in the yellow pages, and verbally spreading word around town as to what I do.

Jeff Fox
*Professional Pianist*

Of course (I've felt discouraged)! I'm only human and my trek has not been easy. I do a great deal of reading to nurture the heart and soul. I surround myself with supportive and positive people (spouse, business partners, employees). I nurture my faith in God and try to remain thankful for everything positive in my life.

Zella Jackson
*Professional Speaker, Consultant, & Author*

When I took on two different jobs that were a huge stretch and I felt like I was going to fail, I shared my anxiety with co-workers and they encouraged me to give it more time. I did and ended up gaining the most meaningful and memorable experiences of my career.

Makenna Perkins
*Marketing and Public Relations Manager*

A lot of rejection comes with being a scientist. I can often remember crying after getting a rejection letter for a major proposal or paper in which I had put in months of work. What I realized then is that if I kept trying, sooner or later the law of averages would help me succeed.

Dr. Richard Radtke
*Research Professor, Oceanography*

My schedule gets a bit overwhelming at times. At such a point I revamp my office area, I review my paperwork flow, redesign forms, prepare for future business more efficiently – I organize! Usually everything falls into place and I note new ideas that helped me handle pressures.

Marcy L. Roberts
*Organizational Consultant*

Many times in the early days of the LYTE Program I really felt like quitting. I even thought of begging my boss to take me back as a Weight Watcher lecturer. It was scary having to start each month with no paycheck guarantees. When the bills came due I often thought it wasn't worth the amount of work to make such meager pay.

The main thing that helped me along with the project were good friends in business who were willing to support me not only morally but financially by giving me business that I desperately needed. I also relied heavily on reading positive books and listening to positive tapes. These things reminded me that others had walked this path before and had made it. I worked hard at believing in the project but mostly believing in myself.

David Tasaka
*Director, LYTE Program*

Any job has elements you may not enjoy, so you have to look at the overall value of the job, even if it's just a paycheck, your job can allow you time to develop your skills and plan ahead for the type of work that would please you more. If I had not been dissatisfied being a lab technician, I might not have moved on to becoming a doctor. I was able to develop some new skills and find a profession that pleases me.

Dr. Cynthia Burdge
*Physician*

*The tricky item for me was
differentiating among the
inner signals that said,*

"Quit and do something else"

*and the signals of caution
and fear that said,*

"Hang in there; don't be a quitter."

*Lots of people feel this ambivalence,
I know. Doing journal writing,
dream work, and actual career
assessment were some of the most
important activities I pursued
to get clear on what to do.*

**Dr. Loren Ekroth**
*Entrepreneur*

*What advice would you give*
*to someone who doesn't think*
*it is possible to enjoy work?*

Be pleased with yourself as you are right now. Almost every job has a few parts that aren't very appealing or fun. I tell my son that it doesn't matter to me what he does (a cook, a baker, a candlestick maker), as long as he does his best and feels good about himself.

Robert Cherry
*Ranch Manager*

Read Joseph Campbell's writings and "Follow your bliss!"

Lynette Cruz
*Angel Network Coordinator*

It is not only possible, it is necessary! Work is one-third to one-half of your life. Get good at something and align yourself with people you respect and enjoy.

Sam Horn
*President, Action Seminars*

Slow down. Take time to evaluate what you are currently doing. Is it satisfying/rewarding/nurturing? Take time to daydream and play "What if?" with as much imagination and heartfelt intent as you can muster. Make time for part time change. Evaluate and enjoy. Then make the big move.

Zella Jackson
*Speaker, Consultant, Author*

I believe that people should enjoy their work and this is accomplished by following their hearts. There is a book entitled, *Do What You Love And The Money Will Follow*. This has always been true for me.

Jeanne Johnston
*World Traveler*

Don't give up! It's your responsibility to find something that you enjoy. Decide what you like to do the most. Don't compromise. List what you like and don't like. Be specific. Be as clear as you can. Then go for it. It's possible. Make sure you're in the career of your choice so you can get what you want out of life. In some careers it's impossible. Be sure you are suited for the career you have in mind. Look to your dream. Where do you want to be in life and will the career help you achieve that end?

Adrian Pacheco
*Hair Stylist*

The best advice might sound a little trite, but I think it is important to think about what you really want, what would make you happy and go out and find your bliss. We are all good at doing at least one thing. The challenge is to find it and to be happy at it. If one ends up doing something which doesn't seem like work, then one is truly blessed.

Richard Radtke
*Research Professor*

I would say to someone who doesn't think that it is possible to enjoy work, that with that attitude, they will be right. I feel that these ideas will become self-fulfilling prophecies of that belief. There is a saying – what you believe, you receive. If a job doesn't turn you on, why stay in it?

David Tasaka
*Director, The LYTE Program*

*In some respects, my handicap
has even been an advantage.*

**Richard Radtke**

*Research Professor*

## RICHARD RADTKE
## RESEARCH PROFESSOR

To many people on campus I am known as the scientist in the wheelchair. This identification is often followed by questions on how I manage to do my research. At one time someone asked me how someone who grew up in Indiana became an oceanographer. It was funny because the first thing that popped up in my mind was, "Have you ever had to feed pigs at 5:00 a.m. in January when it is 20 below zero?" It is a great motivator to want to look for something other than farming.

In college I became interested in ecology and later in fish biology. After realizing that there are more fish in the ocean than in fresh water, I decided to pursue graduate studies in oceanography. After finishing my bachelor's degree in biology at Wabash College, I attended the University of South Carolina. From this time on, I focused on becoming a marine biologist and in getting my Ph.D. I received my doctorate from the University of South Carolina at age 26. I did my post-doc work in Newfoundland, Canada, and subsequently I've been in Hawaii since 1981.

The early part of my career as a scientist, graduate student and post-doctorate, was before the onset of Multiple Sclerosis (MS). I thus had the usual opportunities for early development. This included participation in field expeditions, cruises, and scuba dives, which gave me first-hand experience with these components of research in my field. The onset of MS coincided with the beginning of my career as a researcher at the University of Hawaii. What followed were continuous changes in my life style to adjust to the MS, as I steadily built my research program and my scientific stature in fisheries and oceanography.

To be sure, MS is an inconvenience in any sort of work, but it has not kept me from a normal research career with regular meeting attendance and collaborations. In 1983, and 1986, for example, I was chosen to be a U.S. representative at the international workshops on the Aging of Antarctic Fishes in Orono, Maine and Moscow, USSR, respectively. At present,

I run an active lab with numerous collaborations with colleagues from around the world.

These accomplishments are the result of hard work, dedication, and perseverance. In some respects, my handicap has even been an advantage. Thus, I have developed a research operation which depends on the coordination of many people, colleagues, technicians, and students. It has channeled me into being more of a leader and collaborator then might otherwise have been the case. It has also induced me to utilize technology that I might not otherwise have chosen to apply. The end result has been an expansion of my research program to include the use of new techniques applied to laboratory and field-caught marine organisms from the tropics to the polar seas.

My job tasks range from writing scientific papers to popular articles, and from communicating with scientists to participating in field research. Probably one of my favorite job tasks is writing and doing computer work, although I do get a lot of satisfaction from traveling and doing field work.

The only thing I would probably change is the amount of money that I get paid. Otherwise, I can't think of anything else that I would like to change. I would like more stability in the area of monetary reward, but I enjoy what I do.

The most challenging part is dealing with the criticism and rejection that comes with new ideas and meeting the time limits in which everything is placed.

I didn't have a mentor. I had a lot of perseverance. When people said no and rejected my ideas it made me more inclined to keep at it.

Probably what supported my career growth most is education. I also have a creative and inquisitive nature.

Becoming handicapped is the one event that most impacted my career.

*Security is just a superstition.*
*Life is either a daring adventure*
*or nothing at all!*

**Helen Keller**

*There is a book entitled,*
*Do What You Love*
*And The Money Will Follow.*
*This has always been true for me.*

**Jeanne Johnston**
*World Traveler*

## JEANNE JOHNSTON
## WORLD TRAVELER

I like to think of myself as a world traveler. My passion is traveling. Travel is not only about seeing the sights, but also about meeting people from other cultures. I like to feel the road beneath my feet. I once took off my shoes and walked barefoot down the Left Bank of the Seine in Paris so I could "feel" the ground and know that I had really been there.

This all started with daydreams when I was raising my two children as a single parent. The reality was that I had to work two jobs just to earn a living. Some of my jobs during those years included receptionist and legal secretary.

I wanted to go into management. I attended the College of Travel Industry Management until I applied to Seaflite to do my internship and was hired as their Cabinmate Manager. I had accomplished my goal without a degree.

Some other jobs I had include sales manager for a cruise company, waitress supervisor, and administrative assistant to a promoter who brought to Hawaii such rock stars as Janis Joplin.

When my youngest daughter graduated from high school, I left home! I wanted to travel and did not have the money. So, I made a list of the ten things that I like to do best and put three of them together (boats, cooking and travel) and off I went. The first and one of the most memorable jobs was cooking on a fishing boat in the Bering Sea. I quickly realized that it was far too cold and dangerous to work out on the back deck bleeding cod fish, so I learned to run the boat and navigate and became First Mate!

I was a secretary for a construction company in the Arctic at Prudhoe Bay where the sun went down for almost three months in the winter and stayed up for three months in the summer. In California I was employed as a private investigator where I worked on a homicide case involving a serial murderer. I have also worked as a substance abuse counselor.

Next, I worked as a Chief Steward on several research vessels including those run by the University of Hawaii and Columbia University. Some of the voyages took me to the Bahamas, Brazil, Uruguay, off the tip of South Africa, the Antarctic peninsula, as well as Australia, Indonesia, the South China Sea, the Sulu Sea (where we were boarded by pirates), the Philippines, Guam and many other destinations. Then I worked on tugs which were dragging logs through the Inside Passage and the Alaska Marine Highway. I have also worked on a couple of cruise boats.

What I like best about my "career" is the freedom. I am not a nine-to-five type. My favorite job tasks involve communicating efficiently and effectively, organizing, and logistics. I function well as a trouble shooter and am very project oriented. I have felt discouraged at times because society, in general, does not look upon a person who changes jobs frequently with favor. However, I am highly motivated and know that I must keep on my own path regardless of the opinions of others. I seek out challenges in whatever job I do and try to do the very best I can no matter how mundane the task may seem.

Many people along the way have been very supportive. My children have accepted my lifestyle. I am in the process of growth and change. I need to be creative and this sometimes means changing jobs when the current one gets too routine and I feel my task has been completed. One of the people who has had the greatest impact on me is Helen Keller who said, "Security is just a superstition. Life is either a daring adventure or nothing at all!"

Recently, I have worked as the assistant to the president of a radio station and have run a bed and breakfast in Hilo. I have turned my hobby of photography into a part-time business. I am co-founder and a member of the steering committee of the Hilo Tsunami Museum project. The group includes Dr. Walter Dudley, author of Tsunami. The museum will open in Hilo, Hawaii on April 1, 1996, and our mission is to foster education as well as honor the families and communities affected by past tsunamis. And, there are more exciting jobs out there still waiting for me. I am actually looking for a new project!

*In order to grow,*
*you have to let go.*

**David Tasaka**

## DAVID TASAKA
## DIRECTOR, LYTE PROGRAM

I decided to pursue this work almost by accident. I had been working in the entertainment industry as a booking agent when, after seven years, I decided to do something else but I didn't know what. A friend suggested that I look into working as a lecturer for Weight Watchers since I had been able to maintain my 130 pound weight loss for over eight years at that time.

While working for Weight Watchers, the area manager decided to quit and I applied and got her job. I found that I liked working with people and this field was definitely people oriented. I also found that I brought a lot of empathy to my job since I had once been overweight myself.

I officially started my own company, The LYTE Program, in June, 1985. I had already been teaching the concepts of the program in my Weight Watchers classes and I felt that I wouldn't be able to realize my dream of fully developing these ideas if I stayed with that company.

In the early days, I saw how fortunate I was to have good friends. A friend asked me to conduct a weight management class at her company. When I told her that my materials weren't ready, she said that it was okay and I should make them up as we went along. I cannot overemphasize the importance of having supporters. In the beginning, when there was almost nothing to support except my dream, they came through for me.

My current job tasks are: developing materials, doing classes, marketing the program, taking care of the finances, and any and all aspects of running the company since I am the only full time person on staff. My favorite job is doing the creative work such as creating and marketing new products for the program. I enjoy the many opportunities to meet new people. I also like to write materials for the newsletter, "LYTE Lines." This also gives me ample time to work on my computer which has evolved into a very powerful business tool.

I would like to be able to teach fewer classes and concentrate on creating new systems for duplicating myself. I would also like to get to the point where I could delegate most of the detail work to another staff person.

I started working as a lunch wagon driver in college. When I graduated I started working for a life insurance company the next day. Since I weighed over 300 pounds, I was not very confident and took the first job I was offered. I worked in that industry for four and a half years. Through a series of fortunate circumstances, I was able to lose over 130 pounds during that time. This feat enabled me to move from being an insurance agent into the entertainment business as a booking agent. Even though I had no experience, I created an agency that booked acts all over the world. I think it was then that I came to believe that whatever I really wanted to do, I could do.

I believe that every person has the ability to create a job that they really love. One thing that holds many people back is fear of the loss of security. I have a saying: In order to grow, you have to let go. This has been my motto in life. In the past I spent too much of my life counting on systems outside of myself for security. Since going out on my own I have realized that the only real security is self-created.

The most challenging part of my work is marketing. This is an area that must be worked on constantly. Markets that were once huge can dry up suddenly, therefore, new markets must be sought on an ongoing basis. I believe that those companies who rest on their past laurels will be left behind by their competitors.

I have had many mentors. My definition of a mentor is someone who shows you the path to a better life. There have been friends who listened to me when I was down and out and always said "keep going, you can make it." There were workshop and seminar leaders who gave me ideas which helped me cope with negative challenges. There were friends in business who pointed out mistakes they made so I didn't have to repeat them.

I remember a friend who taught me that the most important asset I had was time, and that I shouldn't waste new time chasing old money. If she had not taught me that lesson, I would have involved myself in a lawsuit which would have totally wiped me out financially and emotionally. Her motto was that if you go into any business, it is like gambling, with the only difference being the game that you are playing.

My career of creating and developing the LYTE Program has been mostly supported by my mother who was there for me emotionally and financially when I started. She believed in my dreams and aspirations. When others thought I was crazy to leave the security of working for a company, she supported my vision of working for myself. I have also been supported by numerous workshops and seminars. The main theme of all of them was for each of us to take total responsibility for our lives. They also taught me that if things were not working out, I could change and make a positive difference in my life.

The event that influenced my career the most was losing 130 pounds and reaching a goal weight. Maintaining that weight loss for the past 23 years has proved to be the major catalyst for my willingness to try new things and to risk living rather than to die at existing. Without my weight loss and weight maintenance, I couldn't be running the type of company that I am running now.

*I found my passion in 1978
when I accepted a job that I didn't
know required public speaking.*

**Pam Chambers**

*Presentation Coach &
Professional Speaker*

## PAM CHAMBERS
## PRESENTATION COACH &
## PROFESSIONAL SPEAKER

I found my passion in 1978 when I accepted a job that I didn't know required public speaking. I wasn't a good speaker and decided to *become* good!

I enjoy speaking on a variety of subjects to all kinds of groups, teaching presentation skills, and working with clients privately to improve their communication skills.

I love the variety and flexibility of my work. However, I need to leverage myself so that I can reach more people who need what I offer. Previous jobs included selling wigs, working on an assembly line, waitressing, and adjusting claims.

I support my career growth by spending time with people who demand more of me than I demand of myself.

My most challenging moment was speaking to 500 unruly teenagers. Nine years of leadership for the Winners' Circle Breakfast Club is the one activity that most impacted my career.

For those wondering how to get into this field, I suggest you seize every opportunity to speak, whether or not you get paid, and keep a list of your engagements. Develop one to three topics. Ask for feedback.

The economy has not affected my business because most people realize that good communication skills are more important than ever!

# CHAPTER TEN

## CREATE WORK YOU LOVE
## AND BE HEALTHY, WEALTHY, HAPPY,
## AND SOMETIMES ALL THREE!

## CHAPTER TEN
CREATE WORK YOU LOVE AND BE
HEALTHY, WEALTHY, HAPPY,
AND SOMETIMES ALL THREE!

A vast majority of those interviewed who love their work did indeed feel good about their annual income. You will read, however, that not all are happy with their earnings. Notice the link so many make between money and happiness. Most of us remember the Beatles' hit, *Money Can't Buy Me Love*. Many are singing the same song, *Money Can't Buy Career Happiness*.

I couldn't find anyone who said, "At first I hated my job. Only took it for the money. After a while, I loved it." Those people might be out there. I just couldn't find any. There seems to be a pattern of starting with happiness.

Read about people who love their work, and about their views on being healthy, wealthy, happy, and sometimes all three!

# HEALTHY

*Did you know that when
you can say "I love my work,"
you reduce your risk of heart disease?
A study done by the Massachusetts HEW
investigating the cause of heart disease
asked participants two questions:*

*Are you happy?
Do you love your work?*

*The results indicated that those
who answered yes have a better chance
of not getting heart disease.*

**Deepak Chopra, M.D.**
*Magical Mind, Magical Body*

*... being in a no-exit and stressful
work situation, loss of job,
lack of education, ...
are all substantial risk factors
for cardiovascular disease.*

**Bernard Lown, M.D.**
*The Antioxidant Revolution*

*It's tragic what happens to people
when they don't like what
they're doing (work).
Ulcers, heart trouble, drinking, etc.*

*It's amazing how many problems disappear when
my clients finally find their niche!*

**Rich White**
*The Entrepreneurs' Manual*

# WEALTHY

### "Are you happy with your annual income?"

Several of the people interviewed who love their work gave the following responses to this question:

One of the results of taking some of the biggest risks in my life is that I now make more money than I ever dreamed of.

Want to double it!

Thank you God for the incredible prosperity in my life and please send more money soon!

I would certainly like to make more money. At this time, however, I think what I do is more important than how much I make.

Yes, I feel really good about my annual income, which this year will be triple or quadruple my income during my last year of university employment.

When you get paid for doing what you love, it's like icing on the cake, and I feel very good about my annual income.

Fantastic.

So far so good; I plan to feel better and better.

Yes, very satisfied.

There's always room to improve.

Absolutely.

My annual income is probably inadequate. Like most people, I sometimes wish it were more, but there are times where I am amazed that I get paid to do something which I really enjoy.

Yes, it is improving steadily.

Although income has been a perk of my work, it is only one of the elements that make my work so satisfying. I think that even if I didn't have to work to make a living, I would still be doing the type of work that I am doing now.

*I have found that those
who are able to do
what they love and
keep themselves focused
on living that way
have the amount of
money they need
come into their lives.*

**Wayne Dyer**
*You'll See It When You Believe It*

When you find a job that's ideal,
take it regardless of the pay.
If you've got what it takes,
your salary will soon reflect
your value to the company.

**Life's Little Instruction Book**


Do what you love and
You'll love what you do
It will show in your work
And your pocketbook, too!

**Makenna Perkins**
*Manager, Public Relations & Marketing*

*But each incarnation, you might say,*
*has a potentiality, and the mission of life*
*is to live that potentiality.*
*How do you do it?*
*My answer is "Follow your bliss."*
*There's something inside you that knows*
*when you're in the center, that knows*
*when you're on the beam or off the beam.*
*And if you get off the beam to earn money,*
*you've lost your life. And if you stay*
*in the center and don't get any money,*
*you still have your bliss.*

**Joseph Campbell**
*The Power of Myth*

*I love meeting new people,
and I feel satisfied that I can be in a place
where I can make someone else happy.*

**Karen Paíkai**

*Restaurant Cashier/Hostess*

## KAREN PAIKAI
## RESTAURANT CASHIER/HOSTESS

"I love my job because of the people I meet. I come from a small family and we're not especially close. At the restaurant customers know me by name and it makes me feel like I belong to a larger family."

Karen works from 7:30 a.m. until 4:00 p.m., Monday through Friday. She enjoys one day off for her birthday and, after 15 years of service, receives four weeks of vacation time each year. Her general responsibilities include working the register, hosting, setting and clearing tables, setting displays, handling invoices and performing some secretarial duties.

"I am left to do my job and I like that. I can spend time thinking about other things while I work. I've always loved being physical indoors and this is one way to do it."

In the course of a day Karen greets between 400 to 500 people, about 75% of whom are regular customers she considers her extended family. The majority of these are retired senior citizens who in turn consider Karen as a family member. She has been invited to birthday parties, graduations, dinners, and weddings through her "family"of friends.

There is an obvious reciprocity in Karen's relationship with her customer-friends. She claims that she receives so much from them, but one sees that she is also able to provide the attention that many elderly people often don't receive. Customers say that an appreciation and love for others comes across when she greets people.

"It's amazing to see so much generosity in people for Christmas and other special occasions. I'll come home with gifts. Customers give me leis, gift certificates and candy. I get so much that I give some away. When someone is kind to me, I want to share this kindness with others."

Problems at work include rude customers, a hectic pace and meager wages. "I may not make a lot of money, but what I earn pays for my small apartment. My children are grown and doing fine. Others may say this job is not challenging intellectually, but that doesn't bother me. I love meeting new people, and I feel satisfied that I can be in a place where I can make someone else happy."

**HAPPY,**

*and sometimes all three!*

*I think it's doing something*
*you love so it doesn't feel like work.*
*You don't think about being disciplined.*
*You do it for the sheer joy of doing it.*
*If you do something you really love,*
*you'll be good at it, and success will follow.*

**Katie Couric**

*Ladies' Home Journal, August, 1992*
*(when asked her formula for success)*

*"I had 16 of the finest, busiest,
most interesting years in the sugar industry.
It was a most technically rewarding experience.
Frankly, I still long to get back to the
sugar fields and visit with the many friends
who helped make that era great."*

**Noel Hanson**
*worked for the Hawaii
Sugar Plantation Association from
1948 to 1964 as a weed control scientist*

*"The man who is happy at his work
is the luckiest man in the world.
One who has the drudge that goes along
each day just to get a few lousy dollars
is a very unfortunate individual.
We were both happy men and still are."*

**Larry McLane**
*Former Manager of Hilo Sugar Company*

*The above lines are from a tape-recorded interview
in March, 1974, of Noel and Larry as they wrap up their
discussion of weed control in Hawaiian sugarcane fields.*

*Noel and Alyce Hanson enjoying
retirement in Cooper Landing, Alaska.*

## Conclusion

Now you have eight steps and many words of wisdom from people who love their work. You're equipped to create work *you* love. What if you try the steps and only make it half way? What if your son or daughter or mother or father become ill and you commit energy to them rather than creating work you love? What if? What if? What if?

Please remember that the purpose of this book is to encourage and inspire you, not to foster guilt. Start when you can. Pat yourself on the back for each step you take. Heal, listen, believe, discover, explore, choose, plan, and balance – all in your perfect time table. You are the boss. This is your book, use it as you wish. If you do only one step, buy a journal. Start listening to the still, wise voice inside you. Record the words you receive. Meditate on the message. May this Love be your guide as you *Create Work You Love*.

# Bibliography

Bolles, Richard, *What Color Is Your Parachute?*, Berkley, CA: Ten Speed Press, updated annually.

Bolles, Richard, *The New Quick Job-Hunting Map*, Berkley, CA: Ten Speed Press, 1990.

Braham, Barbara, *Finding Your Purpose*, Los Altos, CA: Crisp Publications, Inc., 1991.

Campbell, David, *If You Don't Know Where You're Going, You'll Probably End Up Somewhere Else*, Niles, Illinois: Argus Communications, 1974.

Campbell, Joseph, *The Power of Myth*, New York: Doubleday, 1988.

Chopra, Deepak, *Magical Mind, Magical Body*, Illinois: Nightengale Conant Corp., 1990.

Colgrove, Bloomfield, and McWilliams, *How To Survive The Loss of a Love*, Los Angeles, CA: Prelude Press, 1991.

Colozzi, Edward, *Creating Careers With Confidence*, Honolulu: Delta Rainbow, 1984.

Cooper, Kenneth H., *Antioxidant Revolution*, Nashville, Tennessee: Thomas Nelson, Inc., 1994.

Covey, Stephen R., *The Seven Habits of Highly Effective People*, New York: Simon & Schuster, 1989.

Drake Beam Morin, Inc., *Group Career Continuation*, DBM, Inc., 1992.

Dyer, Wayne, *You'll See It When You Believe It*, New York: Avon Publishers, 1990.

Gale, Barry & Linda, *Discover What You're Best At*, New York: Simon & Schuster, 1982

Gawain, Shakti, *Creative Visualization*, New York: Bantam Books, 1979.

Goldsmith, Joel, *The Art of Meditation*, San Francisco: HarperCollins Publishers, 1956.

Hagberg, Janet & Leider, Richard, *The Inventurers*, Reading, Massachusetts: Addison-Wesley Publishing Company, Inc., 1987.

Hazelden, *Each Day A New Beginning*, 1982.

Holland, John, *Making Vocational Choices: A Theory of Careers*, Englewood Cliffs, NJ: Prentice-Hall, Inc., 1973.

Jansen, Dan, *Winning the Mind Game*, USA Weekend, July 15-17, 1994.

Mackay, Harvey, *Sharkproof - Get The Job You Want, Keep The Job You Love In Today's Frenzied Job Market*, New York: HarperCollins Publishers, Inc., 1993.

McGee-Cooper, Ann, *You Don't Have To Go Home From Work Exhausted*, Dallas, TX: Bowen & Rogers, 1990.

Michelozzi, Betty Neville, *Coming Alive From Nine To Five*, Mountain View, CA: Mayfield Publishing Company, 1992.

Miller, Caroline Adams, *Feeding The Soul*, New York: Bantam Books, 1991.

Millman, Dan, *The Life You Were Born To Live*, Tiburon, CA: H J Kramer Inc, 1993.

Mundis, Jerrold, *How to Get Out of Debt, Stay Out of Debt & Live Prosperously*, New York: Bantam Books, 1988.

Naisbitt, John & Patricia Aburdene, *Megatrends 2000*, New York: William Morrow and Company, Inc., 1990.

Occupational Interests Card Sort, San Jose, CA: Career Research and Testing. To order, write: 2005 Hamilton Ave., Ste. 250, San Jose, CA 95125.

*The One Year Bible*, Wheaton, Ill: Tyndale House Publishers, Inc. 1985.

*The Quotable Woman*, Philadelphia: Running Press, 1991.

Robbins, Anthony, *Unlimited Power*, New York: Fawcett Columbine, 1986.

Sher, Barbara, *Wishcraft*, New York: Ballatine Books, 1983.

Siegel, Bernie, *Love, Medicine and Miracles*,
New York: Harper & Row, Publishers, 1986.

Sinetar, Marsha, *Do What You Love, The Money Will Follow*,
Mawhaw, NJ: Paulist Press, 1987.

*This is Michael Bolton*, Sony Music Video Enterprises, 1992.

*Dictionary of Occupational Titles, Occupational Outlook
Handbook,Guide for Occupational Exploration*,
Ask the reference librarian where these sources
for career information are located.

Association for Computerized Systems for Career
Information: Call 703-823-9800 x 309 and ask if your state
has a computerized career information system.

**Sources of Hawaii Occupational Information**
Bank of Hawaii Information and Reference Center -
Visit here if you are interested in researching a local
company -130 Merchant, 11th Floor (537-8518),
8:00am - 5:00pm Bring money for copies and parking.

Career Kokua - Free use of this career information
system updated yearly by the Hawaii State Dept.
of Labor is available at the State Employment Service
830 Punchbowl, #112 (586-8700).

Hawaii State Occupational Information Coordinating
Committee (HSOICC). Call 586-8750 and request a list
of demand occupations in Hawaii.

Call 946-3978 to order the August issue of *The Hawaii
Business* (magazine) which ranks the Top 250 largest
businesses in Hawaii. Cost: $5.00.

Call 596-2021 to order the Pacific Business News *Hawaii
Book of Lists*. Cost: $19.95.

## Dedication to Loren Olson

Dad loved not only his work; he loved life! To celebrate and honor him, the following describes some of the things he did after he was diagnosed with cancer in January of 1989:

JUMPING out of an airplane to do a tandem sky dive in December of 1991.

WEARING an Indian headdress in his hospital bed after his first cancer surgery.

CHECKING out any city's phone book looking for old Navy buddies to call or visit.

CREATING a 50th Wedding Anniversary video by teaming up with a cameraperson and interviewing several family members and friends ... a video we will always cherish.

CATCHING a 55-pound King Salmon on one of his treasured trips to Alaska.

WANTING to start a cancer support group, and using his Indian heritage he so proudly claimed, he would call it the Chemosabe Support Group.

TAKING shark cartilage pills and claiming that soaking in hydrogen peroxide baths improved not only his health, but also his golf game. Some of his friends lovingly called him the "Quick Quack."

DOING hospital visitation; seeking out others with cancer, depression, or whatever, to give support and comfort.

ATTENDING meetings and looking for people who probably didn't get many hugs, and hugging them.

STARTING each day holding mom's hand on the kitchen table saying their morning prayers and devotions.

These are great memories; however, Dad is most inspiring because of his increased faith in a loving God, even after he got cancer. Dad read more books, listened to more tapes, talked to his body, had prayers for healing, and lived longer than anyone his Mayo Clinic doctor had ever seen with his kind of cancer.

**Dad's spirit** is alive and with us. He is complimented by our kind words. He would be even happier if today we hug someone who needs a hug, and re-commit our lives to the loving God that gave him so much Joy, Strength, Comfort and Peace.

Dad's 55 pound
Alaska King Salmon

Dad's tandem
parachute jump

All smiles after
happy landing

*And we know that all that happens to us is working
for our good if we love God, and are fitting into his plans.*
*Romans 8:28*


*If God is on our side, who can ever
be against us? ... For I am convinced that nothing
can ever separate us from his love.
Death can't, and life can't.
The angels won't and all the powers
of hell itself cannot keep God's love away.
Our fears for today, our worries about tomorrow,
or where we are -high above the sky,
or in the deepest ocean – nothing will ever
be able to separate us from the love of God ...*
*Romans 8:31, 38*


*We should make plans –
counting on God to direct us.*
*Proverbs 16:9*


*For I know the plans I have for you, says the Lord.
They are plans for good and not for evil,
to give you a future and a hope ... You will find
me when you seek me, if you look for me in earnest.*
*Jeremiah 29:11-12*


**verses from the**
*Living Bible*

## About the Author

Throughout her career Nancy Hanson has enjoyed a variety of jobs ranging from camp counselor, base camp member of a ski expedition across northern Norway, Finland and Sweden, church youth director, Glacier Queen crew member on Prince William Sound in Alaska, and a full time career counselor since 1988.

As a nationally certified career counselor and President of Career Discovery, she provides career counseling for individuals and groups including those separating from the military. Nancy has taught career development courses for counselors at both Chaminade University and the University of Hawaii. As an outplacement consultant for Drake Beam Morin, Inc., Nancy has worked with clients from corporations including IBM, American Express, Unocal and U.S. Sprint.

Nancy recieved her bachelor's degree from Concordia College, Moorhead, Minnesota, and has a master's degree in counseling and guidance from Pacific Lutheran University in Tacoma, Washington. She is a member of the National Speakers Association and the American Counseling Association. She lives with her husband in Honolulu and has slowly but surely run seven Honolulu Marathons and the 1993 Twin Cities Marathon. She grew up near the farming towns of Hendricks, Minnesota and Astoria, South Dakota.

# To Order Additional Copies of this Book

**Send Postal Orders to:** Career Discovery
1441 Kapiolani Blvd. #2003
Honolulu, Hawaii 96814
(808) 739-9494

**Shipping:** First Class: $2.00 per book

Please mail book(s) to:

Name: _____

Street: _____

City:_____

State: _____

Zip: _____

# of copies

Price:        $10.00  x _____ = _____

Shipping:     $ 2.00  x _____ = _____

                    Total: _____

**Please make
checks payable to:** Angel Network Charities, Inc.*

**Visa and Mastercard accepted**

You may photocopy this page

*A non-profit organization that supports people
in need in Hawaii. Read Lynette's story on pages 79-80
for more information.

# To Order Additional Copies of this Book

**Send Postal Orders to:** Career Discovery
1441 Kapiolani Blvd. #2003
Honolulu, Hawaii  96814
(808) 739-9494

**Shipping:** First Class:  $2.00 per book

Please mail book(s) to:

Name: _____

Street: _____

City:_____

State: _____

Zip: _____

                        # of copies

Price:        $10.00  x  _____  =  _____

Shipping:     $ 2.00  x  _____  =  _____

                        Total: _____

**Please make
checks payable to:**  Angel Network Charities, Inc.*

**Visa and Mastercard accepted**

You may photocopy this page

*A non-profit organization that supports people
in need in Hawaii.  Read Lynette's story on pages 79-80
for more information.